PRAISE FOR *THE BEHAVIOR BREAKTHROUGH*

"*The Behavior Breakthrough* is an outstanding work and a must read for every leader. The combination of behavioral concepts and models along with examples of real world application is exceptional. This book captures a body of knowledge that every person who wants to become a truly great leader must learn. The book is both practical and impactful. I applaud the team at CLG for compiling such a needed piece of leadership guidance. I wish this book would have been available at the beginning of my career."

—*John Kealey, CEO, Decision Lens*

"*The Behavior Breakthrough* provides a clear, no-nonsense approach to achieving real change. Steve Jacobs and colleagues focus on what really matters: how people behave. The tools of applied behavioral science work. It's really that simple."

—*Stewart Thornhill, PhD, Associate Professor, Strategy and Entrepreneurship, and Executive Director, Pierre L. Morrissette Institute for Entrepreneurship, Richard Ivey School of Business*

"Behavior is the essential link between strategy and result, and understanding how to create behavioral change is an essential skill for transformational leaders. *The Behavior Breakthrough* provides excellent coverage of the fundamentals of behavioral science combined with engaging examples from the real world of application. As a client, the approach so clearly outlined in this book was pivotal to creating and sustaining a global organization transformation."

—*William R.K. Innes, retired President, ExxonMobil Research and Engineering Company*

"Many books provide the mental models and knowledge deemed necessary for achieving organizational change. Yet a simple truth remains: 'Knowledge keeps no better than fish.' Despite our best efforts, change, if achieved at all, doesn't last as long as we desire. *The Behavior Breakthrough* verifies a simple truth that, at some level, we have known all along: it is behavior change that drives organizational change and achieves lasting results. Through case studies and an easy-to-understand, common-sense style, *The Behavior Breakthrough* teaches readers how to apply the principles of behavioral leadership to achieve competitive advantage and breakthrough, sustainable results. If you only read one book this year about organizational change, read this one. It's likely to change the way you think about what's important."

—*Jay Strunk, Director, Talent and Development, PPL Corporation*

"*The Behavior Breakthrough* is a tremendous read that provides a very practical and doable behavior-focused approach to achieving improved results. This book provides the education and formula for leading successful change in an easy-to-understand way. For those who require actual proof points before buying in, like me, *The Behavior Breakthrough* specifies what companies have achieved—real value, quantifiable returns, and sustainable higher performance."

—*Pamela Monahan, former VP, Fortune 500 Client*

"One of the most difficult things for a leader is to lead change in his or her organization. Without a guide, the leader can easily become lost in the jungle of existing but unhelpful behaviors, falling back on the familiar favorites of strategy and people. But this book is far more than just a guide; it is an illustrated roadmap, guide, and insightful storyteller all in one. Firmly rooted in the science of behavior, which really appeals to me, it plots a course for the willing leader from the initial idea of changing behavior to get new results, to the El Dorado of behavioral leadership, defining the building blocks and offering the tools and processes to get the job done. It's an invaluable companion for this often difficult journey."

—*Tony McGuire, CEO, System Dynamics (Ireland)*

"To achieve breakthrough performance, you must unlock the power of behavior. The tools and methods I learned from Steve and CLG have made a dramatic impact on my personal and professional performance. *The Behavior Breakthrough* is a must read for any leader seeking to take his or her personal effectiveness to the highest level of performance."

—*Raymond Smithberger, President and General Manager, Individual and Family Plans, Cigna*

"I was first exposed to the DCOM Model and the application of behavioral science to leadership by CLG's Jim Hillgren many years ago. Leadership and talent are the differentiators that separate sustained high-performing companies from the rest . . . and, in our increasingly volatile world, behavioral leadership matters more than ever."

—*Riz Chand, Chief HR Officer, BNSF Railway*

"Delivering higher levels of performance across all levels and functions of the organization is imperative for competitiveness and growth. It is people's actions and reactions that ultimately drive performance. *The Behavior Breakthrough* will set you on the path to understanding how to positively influence your people's actions and reactions."

—*David Murphy, former CHRO, Ford Motor Company and The McGraw-Hill Companies*

"Understanding the behaviors employees need to demonstrate on a consistent basis sustained through effective coaching is critical to achieving a performance breakthrough. The concepts in this book will give leaders a new lever that they may not have considered to successfully execute on their strategy and drive results."

—*Frank Techar, President and CEO, Personal and Commercial Banking Canada, BMO Bank of Montreal*

"*The Behavior Breakthrough* is a must read for the leader who is trying to build a world-class company. Steve and his CLG colleagues have made applied behavioral science—and understanding and motivating human behavior—approachable for the everyday manager. The easy-to-understand tools, processes, and case studies allow the reader to move from a basic understanding of ABS to using behavioral science to drive company-wide performance. In addition, there are clear applications for the healthcare professional who is trying to improve the health of a population through positive behavioral change."

—*Christopher Coloian, President and CEO, Predilytics; Chair, Care Continuum Alliance*

"*The Behavior Breakthrough* lays out the next generation of thinking on effective leadership in a world of accelerating change and competition. The authors unpack incredibly complex ideas into deceptively simple building blocks for game-changing leadership. Committed to getting new results from your team or business? Apply the wisdom contained in *The Behavior Breakthrough*."

—*Jennifer Ciccone, Vice President, Human Resources, Matthews International*

"I have had the privilege of working with some of the finest entrepreneurs in technology over the past thirty years. Each and every one of us can learn from Steve's insights in *The Behavior Breakthrough*. Steve uses the science of behavior to drive actions through to outcomes, versus theory without leverage, which is all too common in business literature. I will be recommending Steve's book to leaders in OMERS Ventures portfolio companies without reservation."

—*Howard Gwin, Managing Director, OMERS Ventures; Corporate Director, BuildDirect; and Chairman, 360incentives.com*

THE

BEHAVIOR

BREAKTHROUGH

*Leading Your Organization
to a New Competitive Advantage*

STEVE JACOBS *and* COLLEAGUES

GREENLEAF
BOOK GROUP PRESS

Published and Distributed by Greenleaf Book Group LLC, www.gbgpress.com
For ordering information or special discounts for bulk purchases, please contact Greenleaf Book Group LLC at PO Box 91869, Austin, TX 78709, 512.891.6100.

The following are registered trademarks or service marks of The Continuous Learning Group, Inc. Behavioral Leadership®, DCOM® Model, Discretionary Performance℠, E-TIP Analysis®, High-Impact Behaviors℠, MAKE-IT® Model, Q4 Leadership℠ Model

Design and composition by Greenleaf Book Group LLC
Cover design by Greenleaf Book Group LLC . Cover image ©istockphoto.com/JuSun.

Cataloging-in-Publication data
(Prepared by The Donohue Group, Inc.)
Jacobs, Steve, 1957-
  The behavior breakthrough : leading your organization to a new competitive advantage / Steve Jacobs and colleagues.—1st ed.
  p. ; cm.
  Issued also as an ebook.
  Includes bibliographical references.
  ISBN: 978-1-60832-418-7
  1. Organizational behavior. 2. Behavior modification. 3. Organizational change. 4. Success in business. I. Title.
HD58.7 .S65 2013
302.3/5   2013931017

Part of the Tree Neutral® program, which offsets the number of trees consumed in the production and printing of this book by taking proactive steps, such as planting trees in direct proportion to the number of trees used: www.treeneutral.com

TreeNeutral®

Printed in the United States of America on acid-free paper

13 14 15 16 17   10 9 8 7 6 5 4 3 2 1

First Edition

To Jim Hillgren,

Our builder of bridge-builders,

Our colleague,

Our friend,

We miss you.

And we thank you for still being here in spirit . . .

➲ CONTENTS

FOREWORD

In 2011, when I became CEO of Cadillac Fairview, we were already one of North America's largest investors, owners, and managers of commercial real estate. Yet behind the scenes, we had become complacent, set in our ways, even a little arrogant. We were still a very good company. I wanted us to be a *great* company.

For that, I needed a call to action. It's hard to motivate people to get behind new directions when things are bad. Even harder when things are already going pretty well.

I chose to focus on improving how leaders across our organization motivated new *behavior* on the job. In commercial real estate, we don't usually think much about competitive advantage through people. We focus mostly on our physical and financial assets. We spend time and energy getting specific properties to yield the best returns. The softer side of business gets ignored. All this together left me unsure that it would work.

But work it has—big time. The "behavior breakthrough," as Steve Jacobs and his colleagues so aptly call it, has made possible a whole new level of performance. Our ability to execute new priorities at Cadillac Fairview has improved in ways that enable us to accomplish things that we simply didn't accomplish in the past. Our culture has improved and our employees are measurably more engaged in their jobs. Best of all, our financial numbers have soared.

It didn't take five years or even three to see an impact. We saw significantly better results—representing an impressive return on investment—*inside of twenty-four months*.

Let me sum it up for you. One of our key competitive advantages in the marketplace used to derive mainly from the strength of our balance sheet. We had an ability to invest in our properties in ways our competitors couldn't. Today, due to the amount of capital available for investment in real estate, that advantage has eroded. But our focus on behavior—on improving our culture and leadership practices—has given us an entirely new advantage.

Changing behavior isn't easy. And building behavioral execution capability like we are doing isn't easy. It requires discipline and determination on the part of senior management. But it's well worth it. If you apply a proven scientific approach, as Steve Jacobs and his colleagues at CLG have for over twenty years, you can take organizations to new heights of executional prowess. *You surpass your competitors because you get better and better at getting things done.*

One area where we made early headway was in changing how we interacted with new tenants in our properties. Learning to collaborate better across our company, we took a process that had long been incredibly (and unnecessarily) hard on our tenants and humanized it. Our tenants today are happier, and we cut the time it took to "onboard" a tenant by several months. That might not sound like a lot, but the cost savings more than paid for our investment in implementing behavioral leadership. Here was a clear and quantifiable result that established for the skeptics among us that focusing on behavior really works.

Many factors contribute to a company's success, but I'm convinced that in today's volatile global economy, the greatest advantage derives from people. We leaders so often underestimate how the everyday habits and behaviors of employees affect the bottom line. That's the bad news. The good news is that a great deal of low hanging fruit is available for the picking using a behavioral approach.

I encourage you to read this book, explore its science, understand its frameworks, and enjoy its case studies. As you move from chapter to chapter, you'll find yourself beginning to see your existing business through new eyes. You'll feel energized and inspired by what is possible. And you'll understand that sometimes the best, most powerful management approaches aren't the flashiest, most technically complex, or the most expensive.

Sometimes they are simple solutions that have been there all along.

John Sullivan, CEO
Cadillac Fairview Corporation
(Leading North American Real Estate Company)
Toronto

ACKNOWLEDGMENTS

Writing a book when you already have a day job inevitably means taking time to write it on the weekends. Substantial time. Time that could otherwise be spent with your loved ones. For this and for many reasons, I thank my family—Jo, Erick, and Cristina—for their patience and sacrifice, not to mention their several creative suggestions about how I could make amends.

My deep thanks go to my colleagues and coauthors. Not only have they contributed to this book; their expertise has immeasurably advanced the body of work in behavioral leadership upon which the book draws.

The cofounders of our company, CLG—Dr. Leslie Braksick, Dr. Julie Smith, and Larry Lemasters—deserve special acknowledgment. This publication coincides with our twentieth anniversary as a firm. Leslie, Julie, and Larry founded CLG upon a simple belief: Companies were becoming better at getting things started, but not at getting things finished. Behavior change mattered, but it wasn't happening, and Applied Behavioral Science could help. That "blue ocean" premise has shaped two decades of groundbreaking practices and, looking forward, the new advantage described in *The Behavior Breakthrough*. Also, our outside directors—Bill Innes, David Murphy, and Patrick Flynn—have provided important executive perspective in further framing this direction.

The book team at our company, CLG, deserves recognition as well. Jamie Berdine helped to conceive *The Behavior Breakthrough* and orchestrated our plan to make it happen. Erica Petrucci quarterbacked the twenty coauthors and scores of weekly milestones for more than a year, and never once compared her task to herding squirrels (at least not audibly). Fred Schroyer generously brought his forty years of publishing experience to the fore, as he has done so many times at CLG. Seth Schulman, our contributing writer on this project, set a new standard for genuine caring and outstanding support. And Donna Dotson deftly managed our calendar demands to ensure that the difficult remained possible.

I'm grateful for the able assistance of our publisher, Greenleaf, and its staff for outstanding editorial, design, and production services.

Finally, I thank our many clients who were quick to see the possibilities of behavioral leadership and bold enough to carve a new path for themselves. We owe them a debt of gratitude, as do their shareholders and employees. It is our privilege to work with them.

Steve Jacobs
Jacksonville, Florida
January 2013

We are what we do repeatedly.
Excellence then is not an act. It is a habit.

—ARISTOTLE

CHAPTER ONE

⊃ THE QUIET REVOLUTION

Steve Jacobs

*It's unbelievable how much you don't know about
the game you've played your whole life.*
—MICKEY MANTLE

What's the secret to superior execution? Is it brilliant strategy? Better processes? Superior technology? No. None of these suffices individually, nor do they suffice in combination. To perform well over the long term, to make everyone's valiant efforts work and "stick," you need another ingredient, something basic and seemingly ordinary: behavior. New results require new behavior. It's that simple—and that difficult.

The Kurrizzo ore-processing facility was a high-tech plant in a third-world setting. The company's new asphalt roadway curved along the river into the dusty community where most workers lived. Fresh paint and flower urns greeted visitors at the office building. But the tranquil appearance was deceiving.

Dodging bullets on the way to the plant wasn't an everyday routine for the workers, but it happened often enough that the workforce was wary.

Tribal conflict plus an unstable government formed the backdrop for the Kurrizzo complex as it sweltered in the equatorial heat.

If there were problems outside the plant, there were plenty inside as well. Safety, reliability, and utilization lagged; the facility was plagued by frequent shutdowns, workplace injuries, and environmental incidents. In addition, lists of action items generated by audits were incomplete, turnover among skilled workers was high, and community relations were poor.

"The Kurrizzo facility has high potential if you can fix it—and we're confident that you're the one to do it, Dave." That's what the executive team members at corporate said when they discussed the assignment with him. "It's your overseas P&L opportunity. If all goes well, you'll be back here in a few years well positioned for your next big step. This assignment will make your career . . . or break it."

Dave parked his Land Rover in the space marked *Ejecutivo Principal* and surveyed the plant as the morning shift changed. It hadn't taken long for him to confirm all the stories he'd heard. An attitude hung in the air, an attitude of "us versus them." Distrust pervaded communication between employees and managers as well as between groups. Employees and contractors flaunted safety rules, striding through the complex without hard hats, safety glasses, or other protective gear. They knew the rules; they simply did not follow them. And production goals were seldom met.

Dave interviewed people to learn the history of employee relations here and formulated a plan with his management team. They launched a back-to-basics campaign to address the conditions that had eroded labor-management trust and people's performance over the years. He and his management team established new processes, stressed the importance of getting the fundamentals right the first time, developed project plans, and emphasized supervisors' responsibility for improving morale. And to ensure clear focus, Dave used benchmarks for world-class performance in similar facilities, and he set targets for improvement in production, safety, reliability, and environmental compliance.

After a lot of hard work, Dave and his team were confident that they had established the right ingredients for a turnaround. *And nothing happened.*

SENIOR LEADER BRIEFING

Early examples in this book are operational, focused on site-level or functional cases of overcoming performance challenges through systematic behavior change. We intentionally start at this level to demonstrate how behavioral leadership works locally, and then progress, in chapters 5 through 10, to the larger strategic implications for business units and the enterprise.

Also, we have been fortunate to collaborate with organizations in diverse industries at all levels, from top executives to managers and supervisors at the front line. Together, we have pioneered a body of work on behavioral leadership that has been two decades in the making. Some of our clients work for best-in-class companies and others for solid but less dominant organizations. Despite their diversity, these organizations share two things: They seek a new source of competitive advantage, and they tell important stories that highlight the connection between behavior and business results. In sharing their stories, we have protected client confidentiality by altering the names of some companies and individuals, and where necessary we have created composite cases. However, we provide unadorned results data so that the results speak for themselves.

More precisely, there were a few positive signs here and there. "It was a start," Dave recalled, "but not enough. After six months, safety hadn't improved, and our environmental violations were increasing. Worse still, we'd suffered a serious fire and plant shutdown. Attitudes had begun to improve, but performance had not."

Employees and managers still put production ahead of safety and environmental concerns, and managers still used many of the same leadership practices—which had become leadership habits—that had been in place for years. When Dave asked colleagues why nobody heeded safety procedures, they replied wistfully, "You can't expect them to worry about hard hats and work safety when they're worried about getting shot on the way home."

Here, then, was a mission-critical initiative that should have succeeded but didn't—*all because Dave and his team had neglected the daily, ingrained behavior of plant workers and managers.* Dave and his team had worked hard and meant well, and they assumed their actions would lead automatically to new employee behavior. They didn't. Dave had left to chance the crucial ingredient of *changing people's behavior.*

How much more effective and profitable might their efforts have been had Dave and his team worked to change employees' behavior systematically? How much more progress could they have made by improving their own skill in motivating the behavior change that the plant needed?

BEHAVIOR: THE NEGLECTED GAME-CHANGER

This book introduces you to a neglected game-changer in the world of business: *Behavioral Leadership*®. Behavioral leadership focuses on crafting desirable shifts in everyday habits, behaviors, and routines. Based on *Applied Behavioral Science*, a discipline that has been researched and taught in major universities for decades, behavioral leadership puts to work the principle that *new results require new behavior*, and significant new results—those that confer a broad and significant competitive advantage—require the *right* new behaviors, and the right *few* behaviors, that endure over time.

Unfortunately, almost all organizations overlook the essential role that *targeted behavior change over time* plays in achieving superior results. As a result, promising new initiatives never get off the ground or stall in midair, resulting in wasted resources and subpar performance. Consider the following:

- A market-leading insurance company painstakingly analyzes the best practices of its highest-performing salespeople, holds dozens of

APPLIED BEHAVIORAL SCIENCE

Behavioral science explains human *behavior*: why we do what we do, say what we say, or don't act at all. Behavioral science has the same properties as other natural sciences like chemistry and biology: careful observation, data collection, reliability of occurrence, replicability, measurability, laws, and rigor. The science has matured through nearly a century of research.

Today we apply Behavioral science to improve the performance of leaders, organizations, and employees. Applied Behavioral Science is a powerful and enduring way to achieve sustainable business results, and it underpins a reliable, replicable technology for managing behavior and implementing change.

---

meetings to spread these best practices throughout the sales force—and nothing happens. Some salespeople attempt a few of the practices, but not consistently, not completely, and not for very long.

- A mining company invests in state-of-the-art handheld electronic trackers so its employees can improve equipment reliability—and nothing happens. Their main reliability metric—Mean Time Between Failures (MTBF)—doesn't budge, and the company doesn't realize the considerable cost savings it had anticipated.

- An equipment manufacturer redesigns its operations from start to finish to better compete with foreign manufacturers, deploying the smartest teams and the best designs—and again, you guessed it, nothing happens. The project bogs down because line employees continue to perform their jobs in the same inefficient and unhelpful ways.

Each of these real-life organizations expended considerable resources getting strategy, process, and technology right, yet they stopped there, leaving to chance everyday behaviors on the part of workers, managers, and leaders. The chronically disappointing performance that followed had smart, well-meaning executives scratching their heads, wondering what else they could do to move the needle.

These are not isolated examples. One recent study found that nearly 80 percent of strategic initiatives fail to achieve their goals, according to the executives who sponsor them, with 40 percent of the potential return left on the table. A 2008 *Harvard Business Review* survey of 125,000 participants at companies in more than fifty countries found that three out of every five companies rated their organization as weak at execution. Yet another study found that 64 percent surveyed did not believe their companies would close the gap between their strategies and their ability to execute them.

SOFT STUFF? ASK THESE CEOS . . .

Behind these numbers lurk some familiar attitudes. Most executives disregard behavior and related subjects like leadership skills and culture because they view them as "soft stuff." Executives seeking to improve field sales performance, for instance, might hire new salespeople or design a new field sales compensation system, but they generally don't emphasize what the field sales managers can *do* differently, or what top performers are *doing* that others are not.

To understand how deep leaders' prejudices run, consider what happened at a forum of thirty Irish technology CEOs. The Irish government had challenged the CEOs to achieve five to ten times growth in export turnover (i.e., revenue growth in international sales) and had invited them to participate in an executive program custom-designed by Stanford University's Graduate School of Business. A number of the executives were reluctant to leave their businesses three times within a year for a full week, and they were very pointed in their demand for real-world topics of practical value, like strategy, mergers and acquisitions, and international finance. Also, they were very clear that they wanted to avoid "fluff."

At the end of the first week, the group did something unusual. It was a Friday night, but rather than take time off, executives reconvened in the classroom where they were spending long daytime hours. The CEOs decided to review each of their respective thirty companies and identify which topics, out of the several they had covered that week, provided the most significant competitive advantage for accelerated international growth. One by one, the CEOs stood at the whiteboard and checked off topics that had personally resonated with them.

A surprising pattern emerged. Two—and only two—of the more than a dozen topics were identified by all thirty CEOs as most relevant to accelerated growth for their company: *leadership* and *culture*.

This news occasioned an audible gasp among those in the room. These executives had arrived a week earlier very clearly focused on strategy, international selling, and other topics they considered to be the "meaty," important stuff. They certainly didn't expect to conclude that topics like leadership and culture, which relate to how people behave, would serve as their most important drivers going forward.

THE MISSING CAPABILITY: BEHAVIORAL LEADERSHIP

Companies have it in their power right now to create leadership habits and cultural conditions that drive superior results. Yet given ingrained attitudes, it comes as no surprise that most executives don't—or can't—shape their own behavior or others' behavior very well.

BEHAVIORAL LEADERSHIP IS . . .

. . . the business discipline of fostering and sustaining people's Discretionary Performance^{SM} of High-Impact Behavior^{SM} to achieve unparalleled results. Scaling this discipline across leaders and applications drives superior execution and, ultimately, competitive advantage.

In 2008, Lominger International surveyed 4,200 leaders around the globe to discover how leadership competencies and priorities varied by region. The most prominent general finding: *Strengths and weaknesses in leadership skills were much more similar than different.* Out of sixty-seven competencies, seven of the ten weakest (highlighted in Figure 1) were all-important leadership behaviors such as "motivating others," "confronting direct reports," and "managing vision and purpose." Coming in dead last was "developing direct reports and others."

Top 10 (Strongest) Competencies	Bottom 10 (Weakest) Competencies
Integrity and trust	Innovation management
Ethics and values	Managing through systems
Intellectual horsepower	Understanding others
Functional/technical skills	Confronting direct reports
Action-oriented	Motivating others
Perseverance	Dealing with paradox
Customer focus	Conflict management
Approachability	Managing vision and purpose
Standing alone	Personal learning
Managing diversity	Developing direct reports and others

Source: K.P. DeMeuse, K.Y. Tang, K.J. Mlodzik, and G. Dai, "The World Is Flat . . . And So Are Leadership Competencies," Lominger International, June 2010.

Figure 1. Global competencies study of 4,200 leaders

The Lominger International study of global leaders highlighted another finding: Managers rated themselves as being more skillful than their coworkers did. Researchers summarized this result by citing a 2007 *Businessweek* article stating that "90 percent of managers think they're among the top 10 percent of performers in their workplace." Having worked with 360-degree feedback data from Fortune 100 companies for more than two decades, we can attest to the pronounced tendency of leaders to overrate themselves.

Even when leaders do recognize their weaknesses in shaping new behavior, they don't improve unless they apply conscious effort; in fact, none of us do. In 2004, Dr. Edward Miller, dean of Johns Hopkins University School of Medicine and CEO of their hospital, gave a talk at a private conference at Rockefeller University, the New York City medical research center. As he related, a number of research studies had investigated how well coronary bypass patients adhered to diet and exercise regimens designed to prevent the need for another (very painful) surgery. The research found that 90 percent of patients had returned to their prior unhealthy habits within eighteen months.

No, that is not a typo: *90 percent!* In the workplace and throughout our lives, instances in which people know what behavior is desirable in a situation, but choose to do something else, are so commonplace that they frequently escape our notice.

A NEW COMPETITIVE ADVANTAGE

The widespread neglect of behavior in organizations creates a tremendous opportunity for transformative business leaders—those elite few who are willing to invest the time, focus, and energy to do something new to achieve something great. John Sullivan, CEO of Cadillac Fairview, a premier Canadian commercial real estate company, puts the opportunity this way:

> Our industry competes on tangible things like physical assets, capital investments, and acquisitions. None of our competitors are thinking about behavior as a source of competitive advantage. And even if they were, we have a head start that we don't intend to relinquish. [Behavioral leadership] will put new distance between us and them for years to come.

Everyday behavior is so important—and so neglected—that in the years ahead, competitive advantage in any industry or geography will flow as much from behavioral leadership as from new strategies, processes, or technologies. In fact, *behavioral leadership techniques will get your existing strategies, processes, and technologies working to their full potential by reducing the hidden human barriers that so often scuttle them.*

In a global business environment, disciplined attention to behavior will also help businesses solve and avoid disruptive cultural clashes. As more businesses turn to innovation as a path to growth, a focus on behavior will help companies embed deep cultures of creativity and openness on the ground level, enabling innovation to persist over time.

In effect, the decades-old science of behavior has the potential to trigger a *quiet revolution* in companies that apply it. We use the term *revolution* because for many companies, behavioral leadership is a fundamental shift in focus that leads to significant shifts in performance. Though subtle, behavioral leadership is a catalyst for profound new insight that drives new action and new results.

This revolution is a quiet one nonetheless. Behavior change prowess isn't flashy and it isn't likely to capture headlines like other advances such as, say, genomics or nanotechnology. Behavior change isn't instant or effortless (though first-year returns are routinely extraordinary). And practitioners are not eager to publicize this source of advantage precisely because, as one senior leader put it, "this really, really works!" For a growing number of companies, however, the fact that behavioral leadership is flying below the radar is part of its appeal.

The transformation afforded by behavioral leadership is no less sustainable or lasting for being so quiet. Quite the contrary. Competitors often match pricing strategies quickly, buy themselves the new technology that has given lift to the first adopter, and duplicate others' lean processes within months. But as John Sullivan points out, they have to *develop* the ability to foster and leverage behavior, and this takes time and focus. The more competitors try to take shortcuts, the longer it will take them.

Revolution is a dramatic word, but here it's appropriate. In the few leading-edge companies that have applied it, behavioral leadership has helped them avoid executional miscues and attain game-changing increases in value. Consider the following:

- One major airline saw an 85 percent jump in customers' intent to repurchase—especially helpful at a time of financial challenges for the company.

- A large hospital was able to roll out a technological innovation in only ten days, as opposed to the historical track record of three years, resulting in impressive savings in time and cash.

- A health-care insurance company saw a key measure of customer experience improve an average of 26 percent while return on investment for building the behavioral leadership capability was 438 percent within the first eighteen months.

These are not isolated examples. In the next chapter, we'll describe some of the spectacular returns a few leading-edge companies across industries and geographies have already realized, including superior execution, highly engaged employees, and sustained business impact.

We've designed the rest of the book to explain these results to you and to suggest how you can achieve similar ones for your own company. Chapters 3 and 4 take you behind the scenes, exploring what innovative leaders have come to understand about behavior, while chapters 5 through 9 convey how these leaders' new understanding has helped them alter core business processes and functions for better performance and profitability. Chapter 10 reveals how behavioral leaders are extending this capability throughout their organizations to sustain high performance and seize new competitive advantage over the long term.

A number of executives with whom we work strongly prefer "substance over sizzle," and this principle guides *The Behavior Breakthrough*. Grounded in hard science, the book offers scores of real-life examples of notable companies that have applied behavioral leadership and achieved significant successes. Our goal: to provide a comprehensive, detailed, and reader-friendly introduction to applying behavioral leadership in proven and practical ways.

A BEHAVIORAL LEADER SPEAKS

BILL INNES, INTERNATIONAL EXECUTIVE FOR SEVERAL DIVISIONS OF A FORTUNE 10 COMPANY

During more than thirty years of running businesses worldwide, I assumed that clear strategies and bright people were all I needed for success. And I was consistently disappointed.

My aha moment came in a conversation with CLG's Leslie Braksick. As we discussed how I could leverage new performance levels from our corporation's merger, and how having strategy and good people weren't enough, I suddenly realized that strategy is transformed into results only when people *do* something—when they behave differently. I recognized that behavior is the essential link between strategy and getting results.

Behavioral leadership elevates performance to a whole new level by focusing on specific behaviors needed for success and how to make them happen. Behavioral leaders must set the example. You cannot ask people to behave in a way that you are not prepared to do yourself.

In addition to producing exceptional business results, behavioral leadership provides a much more satisfying working context for people because it aligns what they actually do with what their organization is trying to achieve, and from this they experience the strong satisfaction that they are making worthwhile contributions.

I'm now retired, and in my work as a CLG executive adviser I am using my experience with behavioral leadership to help others create better results and better working environments for people in their organizations.

THE POWER OF YOUR NEW EYES

French novelist Marcel Proust once observed, "The real voyage of discovery lies not in seeing new landscapes, but in having new eyes." Applied Behavioral Science and the behavioral leadership discipline are powerful in part because they allow leaders to reassess their own vexing business challenges with *new eyes*. This new insight drives new action and new results.

Remember Dave's challenge from the beginning of this chapter? Behavioral leadership methods enabled him and his team to identify the key behavior changes that would accelerate business performance as well as the leadership skills and processes most essential to encouraging this behavior change. Leaders were able to see through new eyes what was keeping employees from acting as owners and operators of their business, and they were able to chart and implement a fundamentally new path.

Dave and his team first acknowledged that the inconsistent plant results owed ultimately to inconsistent behavior among frontline employees *as well as* supervisors and leaders. Next they examined why this inconsistent behavior was occurring, and they found that the existing behavior made sense *from the perspective of plant personnel*. Although the senior team had communicated safety, reliability, and environmental compliance as top priorities, other actions of theirs implied that production was the real number-one concern.

Moreover, employees felt confused about what "critical few" behaviors were most important each day, in part because nobody had explicitly identified these behaviors. Senior leaders expected supervisors and managers to build a spirit of commitment and ownership within the plant, but the latter often felt more comfortable with a command-and-control style and lacked the new skills required. Seldom did supervisors and managers offer positive encouragement for a job well done, and seldom did they emphasize preventing problems rather than fixing them once they had occurred.

Armed with this insight, Dave's team moved to develop and apply behavioral leadership capability. Building upon their long-term objective of "The Perfect Day," they adopted as their priority incident-free operations, meaning zero incidents relating to employee safety, environmental emissions, and plant reliability. To achieve these results, the team established high-impact behavior targets for employees, including identifying and acting upon potential risks each day. And, knowing that successful problem prevention requires that employees feel strong ownership and exercise good judgment (rather than merely going through the motions), Dave and his team established employee engagement targets accordingly.

The leadership team worked with managers and supervisors to craft behavior change plans within each area of the plant as well as to develop new skills among managers and supervisors (starting with themselves) to motivate *want to do* performance. Frontline supervisors, for instance, identified a new, high-impact practice for themselves, namely to facilitate a discussion about "Where might we be at risk today?" in every shift turnover meeting. Supervisors also identified new practices for themselves when problems in the plant *did* occur. Rather than merely high-fiving their fixing of the problem, they acknowledged employees' contributions in problem correction, but then led a discussion of "What can we learn from this so that we prevent it next time?" The behavior change plans then captured supervisors' plans to encourage increasing *want to do* performance of prevention behaviors and to make this business as usual.

What happened? Within nine months, 90 percent of the plant's managers and supervisors had performed their targeted behaviors, and nearly that many had attained targeted results. Frontline supervisors and middle managers were successfully adopting practices to positively influence behavior in the desired direction. And the results spoke for themselves:

- Environmental incidents decreased by nearly three-fourths.
- Safety improved by over half.

- Production increased by nearly half.
- Lost-profit incidents decreased by three-fourths.
- Employee commitment rose by nearly three-fourths.
- Union grievances disappeared.

Dave was so impressed by the turnaround that he wrote a letter to the entire plant:

> It hardly seems possible that just one year ago we were an organization in firefighting mode (figuratively and literally!). The positive changes that have been accomplished are nothing short of sensational in such a short time. Not only is the plant running better, safer, and at a lower cost, but the atmosphere in the workplace is different. People are much more engaged, the place is cleaner, people are taking on tasks willingly, and true ownership is beginning to sprout . . . Without your support and guidance our journey would have been much harder and longer. On behalf of everyone at the plant—thank you for a job well done.

As Dave's experience illustrates, the practice of behavioral leadership opens up new possibilities—with untold benefits for you, your company, all who work there, and even your customers. *Your existing strategies, processes, and technologies will work better than ever before because you've eliminated human barriers that have impeded them all along.*

WHAT THE BEST WILL DO

This book is for innovative leaders who seek competitive advantage that cannot be easily replicated—leaders who value substance over flash, and who are comfortable pushing into their discomfort zone knowing that's what it takes to perform to the fullest. You know who you are: a determined game-changing leader who *does* things beyond the norm in order to *achieve* things beyond the norm. A leader who intentionally improves and makes yourself vulnerable, challenging your own ingrained beliefs about performance, behavior, and leadership. If you're interested in what works rather than merely what's new, this book is for you.

Information today is everywhere and instantaneous, but practices as simple as meaningful feedback between leaders and employees or consistent task performance are still as scarce as ever. Bringing new everyday behaviors into your organization can prove more useful and more conducive to an energized, engaging work environment than any strategy or process you might embrace. We also hope that your new perspective will lead in short order to meaningful changes in your leadership practices and your organization's programs and policies, as it has for many of the leaders and companies profiled in this book.

When you finish this book, you will not only possess a new path to competitive advantage, but the tools and knowledge to help your employees consistently deliver the *want to do* performance that drives new advantage. You will feel empowered to do a leader's true work better than ever, with new confidence, competence, and ambition. You will go home each night knowing that you have made a positive difference in the lives of others. And you will forge a legacy by turning the common sense of behavioral leadership into what companies everywhere most need it to be: *common practice.*

⟳ *THE BEHAVIORAL LEADER'S SNAPSHOT SUMMARY*

In brief:

- Behavior is a powerful performance lever.
- Behavioral leadership enables leaders to see new possibilities that lead to new action and new results.

- Organizations that have learned to use this lever well consistently achieve extraordinary business impact.

- This capability can be used as sustainable competitive advantage. It is at the heart of superior execution.

- The behavioral leadership advantage is unique and is unlikely to be commoditized by competitors.

Ask yourself:

☐ Do we systematically prioritize and manage behavior change with the same emphasis that we place on strategy, process, and technology?

☐ Do we do this well?

☐ Do we sustain the gains from behavior change?

CHAPTER TWO

➲ YOUR RETURN ON REVOLUTION

Steve Jacobs, Annemarie Michaud, Brian Cole, and Dee Conway [1]

The dollars are worth more when I can predict them.
— JACK STACK, CEO AND AUTHOR [2]

In our everyday lives, we intuitively understand that new results require new behavior, and that disciplining ourselves to behave in new ways can allow us to improve performance. Golfers seeking to improve their putting may experiment with new equipment, but sooner or later they succeed by adopting different behavior, such as changing their grip or adjusting their backswing. Likewise, behavioral leaders understand the very real return that behavior yields—what we call the *Behavior* → *Results connection*. They invest accordingly and, when necessary, capture data demonstrating the measurable impact.

This chapter explores the financial and nonfinancial returns that harnessing this connection can produce. It describes the "new math" now emerging around behavioral leadership and presents tips for senior leaders intent on funding investment in behavioral leadership. All management approaches promise ample returns, but as we shall see, behavioral leadership really does begin and end with business impact.

BIG RETURNS ON THE REVOLUTION

When behavioral leaders skillfully pursue behavior change, results follow even in seemingly impenetrable problem areas. *The Behavior Breakthrough* provides numerous examples ranging across industries, performance dimensions, continents, and functions:

- An industrial company achieved half a billion dollars in logistics cost improvements within two years (among other key results) by embedding behavioral leadership practices in its annual plan deployment process (chapter 5).

- A research laboratory achieved unprecedented levels of engagement, productivity, and customer delivery—despite painful layoffs— by utilizing behavioral leadership approaches for organizational change (chapter 7).

- A major mining operator achieved improvements exceeding 200 percent in safety and nearly $400 million in cost savings in two years, yielding about 30:1 return on investment (ROI), by applying behavioral leadership processes for transforming an entrenched, underperforming culture into a culture of ownership and accountability (chapter 8).

- Canadian National Railway tripled its stock price in four years while applying similar behavioral leadership processes for building a culture of "precision railroading" (chapter 8).

- iDirect Technologies, a designer of satellite-based broadband access solutions, grew from the brink of bankruptcy to a $120 million entrepreneurial front-runner within three years by applying behavioral leadership practices to everything from influencing leasing terms to keeping the doors open to accelerating customer purchasing decisions (see "A Behavioral Leader Speaks" in chapter 3).

- A business unit of a Fortune 50 industrial company achieved five consecutive years of profit improvement and a sixteenfold improvement in safety by enhancing the behavioral leadership acumen of the unit president and his leadership team (chapter 9).

- A manufacturing plant of a leading pharmaceutical company achieved a half-billion dollars in improvements in productivity and won corporate awards for "best overall business improvement" by integrating behavioral leadership and Lean Six Sigma processes.

These examples represent only a sampling of the instances in which leaders have exploited the Behavior → Results connection to achieve remarkable results. In one industry alone—manufacturing—companies have applied behavioral leadership to achieve numerous beneficial results and yield dramatic returns (Figure 2).

IMPROVEMENT AREAS	RESULTS
Reliability	• 325% increase in critical preventive maintenance performance • 75% drop in unplanned shutdowns
Productivity & Utilization	• 92% record utilization led to record high-value product yield, adding $40 million to profits • Capacity rose sharply in one year on three production lines: 88%, 107%, 105%
Safety	• 75% decrease in recordable incidents over 6 months • 27% increase in compliance with use of Personal Protection Equipment (PPE)
Cost Management	• $380 million savings within two years • 45% drop in one year in equipment rental and hauling costs
Quality	• 50% increase on one production line with 15% less variability • 78% drop in exception on operators' recording of equipment data
Environmental Excellence	• Reduced environmental incidents 25% below targeted goal • Environmental exceedances dropped two-thirds in 6 months
Employee Engagement	• Morale index improved 70% in 6 months • Employee commitment index moved from "worst" to "first"

Figure 2. Examples of behavioral leadership impact in manufacturing companies

THE GOOD CAN GET EVEN BETTER

Behavioral leadership can enhance performance even in organizations that are already running at the top of their game. Consider what happened at a global chemical company's top-performing plant. While the plant's team was working to build behavioral leadership into its operations, corporate announced an immediate 10 percent cost-reduction mandate. The plant had already spent two years improving performance and cutting costs. Now, to the chagrin of many on-site, they were receiving the same mandate as everyone else.

Turning to the numbers, the plant manager advocated one new area for improvement: reducing unplanned shutdowns. Chemical plants rely on large amounts of equipment that can fail if not properly maintained. One failed pump can hamstring production, costing millions a day.

Team members protested that they had addressed this issue for more than thirty years. They'd implemented quality initiatives, Six Sigma, and new technologies. What more was there?

"Let me ask you this," the plant manager said, "if every person in operations and maintenance, every day and every shift, were to do all the right things, would we still have the rate of unplanned shutdowns that we are experiencing today?"

"Well, no," his colleagues responded, "but again, we've done everything we know how."

The plant manager kept pushing. "But if the answer is to get everyone to do the right things, that's about behavior. Isn't that what we're here to learn more about?"

They began brainstorming the right behaviors that people in maintenance and operations could perform every day to avoid unplanned shutdowns. The list ballooned until the team said, "Whoa—we can't have people focus on all these things. Which one or two behaviors could we start with?"

At that point, a thirty-year veteran who previously had been silent slapped his hand on the table. "I'll tell you what people need to do—they need to listen! Anyone who has been around here as long as I have knows you can hear equipment problems coming, if you know what to listen for." This insight helped the management team turn the corner. From their list of twenty-five-plus behaviors, they identified two high-impact behaviors on which to focus:

1. Each person in operations and maintenance would take five minutes, twice per shift, to visit designated plant areas and listen, then record what they heard on a clipboard. If they heard anything suspicious, they would alert a supervisor.

2. Teams would rehearse the immediate response procedure at each shift turnover, enabling everyone to be current on roles and accountabilities should something occur.

By year's end, despite thirty years of steady progress toward reducing unplanned shutdowns, the plant further decreased the unplanned shutdown rate by an astonishing 75 percent. That was worth about $50 million annualized. The potential when scaled across the company's nearly two dozen additional plants was, of course, even more significant.

VALIDATING THE EVIDENCE

It's easy to throw around numbers. Do we really know if these new results owed to the new, targeted behaviors?

The Kurrizzo ore-processing plant mentioned in chapter 1 conducted extensive statistical analysis and demonstrated strong and significant correlations between changes in behavior and changes in targeted results.[3] As the plant manager noted:

> The statistical analysis quantifies conclusions that were readily apparent to those of us who worked at the plant . . . Our results improved primarily because people's behaviors changed. And people's behaviors changed because our frontline supervisors knew precisely what

people (including themselves) needed to do differently to get the improved results. To me, one of the most satisfying outcomes was the improvement in employee commitment index [from under 50 percent to nearly 80 percent], which bodes well for continued improvement in all of the key areas.

This manager had evidence that the correlations owed to behavioral leadership practices and not other factors because the behavior change plans preceded actual behavior change, actual behavior change preceded results improvements, and other factors were ruled out by events and statistics. The behavior changes took place in two distinct phases over a number of years, and in each case, the phase of higher performance coincided with a period in which the plant implemented behavioral leadership practices.

In an information technology company, a similar analysis also verified the link between results and behavioral leadership. Leaders' engagement in a particular type of performance coaching (described in more detail in chapters 6 and 8) increased high-impact performer behaviors, which in turn significantly improved targeted results. Completing what company leaders called their "virtuous cycle," the analysis demonstrated that improvement in results then led to significantly increased leadership engagement in performance coaching, which was key to sustaining the gains over time.

In yet another case, a large US health-care insurance company had been struggling to provide the kind of high-quality customer service so essential in their industry for retaining customers. They applied behavioral leadership to improve customer service quality. The result: an average 26 percent improvement in their customers' claims and call experience. The ROI for developing the initial behavioral leadership capability was 438 percent within the first eighteen months. The company reversed large-market erosion and bolstered their share value. Improvements in customer service, worth tens of millions, clearly corresponded to systematic changes the company made in the high-impact behaviors they had identified.

Nor did the benefits end with the immediate financial impact. By the mid-2000s, the company's service ranking among the top ten North American health insurers had moved from last to first. The company became the first in their industry to receive the J.D. Power customer excellence award. Quite unexpectedly for this enterprise of more than 40,000 people, employee engagement scores for service operations jumped from their long-standing dead-last position to company-leading levels.

Additional analysis of this unprecedented leap confirmed that the advances owed to changes in the behavioral leadership practices adopted by service-operations managers.

But, could company leaders be sure that these results were really attributable to the behavioral leadership applications and not to other factors? After all, they had introduced new technology, restructured, hired scores of new managers, and provided new basic skills training. The answer is yes, again. Comparing pairs of skillful strong-adopter behavioral leaders with weak-adopter counterparts who reported to the same boss and who experienced all other organizational improvements in common, we found a 255 percent improvement advantage for strong adopters. This difference was replicated in three separate analyses over five years.

THE NEW MATH OF BEHAVIORAL LEADERSHIP

As we saw in chapter 1, many companies perceive leadership and behavior as intangible, difficult to measure, and less essential to financial performance than other drivers. Moreover, managers regard efforts to improve behavior as costs that must be contained rather than as investments that can be commercially leveraged. For instance:

- Few companies estimate the value of potential performance lift that the right type of employee engagement might deliver, much less invest toward this with clear ROI targets and time frames.

- For leadership skills initiatives, companies do not typically measure the leading indicators (e.g., number of feedback discussions per direct report per month) or lagging results (e.g., percentage increase in productivity or profitability).

- Companies implementing strategic initiatives typically do not measure the extent to which individuals are adopting them, nor do they estimate the ROI of further effort to increase adoption rates.

- When companies do achieve measurable results, they don't invest specifically to sustain the gains.

As behavioral leaders become more sophisticated, they begin to adopt new approaches for estimating potential ROI and deciding when, where, and how long to invest in behavioral capability. We touch on four of these methods here:

- The Cost of Leadership Neglect

- The Cost of Partial Adoption

- The Value of Sustainability

- The Value of Capability Extensions

Cost of Leadership Neglect

Building upon a concept first introduced by Alfred Guiffrida and Rakesh Nagi[4] regarding the "Economics of Managerial Neglect," *cost of leadership neglect* captures the opportunity cost of *not* systematically developing behavioral leadership skillfulness throughout a business unit or enterprise.

It is one thing for a leadership team to weigh a budget expenditure of X dollars for developing leadership capability in the coming year, and quite another for the leadership team to knowingly reject the opportunity to save (or generate) five to fifteen times that amount per annum.

In its early pilots, the health-care insurance company mentioned earlier found that developing skillful behavioral leadership practices yielded a return in excess of five times in productivity and cost-of-poor-quality savings. Conservatively, this represented a potential annual recurring savings of $23 million for the budget-constrained service operations unit. Once managers understood the extent of the actual savings, discussion shifted from the cost of behavioral skills development to the money the company would leave on the table each year by not applying behavioral leadership practices.

Cost of Partial Adoption

A second example of the new math of behavioral leadership is the *cost of partial adoption.* So often, companies roll out strategic initiatives—from skills training to technology implementations, merger integrations to cultural transformations—without clear metrics for establishing how extensively people are adopting a desired behavior. Even if the company achieves its goals in the aggregate, the incremental gain that would accrue with more complete adoption typically goes unnoticed.

Behavioral leaders look at adoption differently. Since adoption is new behavior, and we can measure both new behavior and its *value,* we can decide when it makes sense to invest further in incremental adoption and when the likely yield reaches the point of diminishing financial return.

Despite the strong ROI that the service operations unit in the health-care insurance company described previously achieved in its first implementation cycle, closer scrutiny revealed that only 50 percent of leaders had fully adopted behavioral leadership skills to date. Another 40 percent were partial adopters, while 10 percent were nonadopters. Having estimated the differential performance of strong adopters, senior leaders could calculate that boosting adoption rates from 50 percent to 80 percent would yield an incremental ROI of nearly six times!

Value of Sustainability

A third example of behavioral new math is the *value of sustainability.* Remember the last time you dieted to reach your target weight and vowed to yourself that this time you would keep the weight off? Unfortunately, most companies and many leaders tend to assume that any change their organization makes will stick, and so they shift their time and attention to other things. Behavioral leaders understand that shaping new behavior is essential but *sustaining* behavior change yields the greatest prize. They explicitly estimate ROI on the sustainability investment and plan accordingly.

Using such an approach, the health-care insurance company's service operations unit identified key sustainability processes such as monthly sustainability discussions at standing team meetings, quarterly sustainability checks, and skills coaching for new managers. While these activities certainly required time and budget, they comprised a fraction (less than 20 percent) of the initial investment and would yield an expected ROI of seventeen times, even without considering continuous improvements beyond the initial results impact.

Value of Capability Extensions

Fourth, behavioral leaders calculate the *value of capability extensions.* The greatest return on investments in behavioral leadership comes from new applications of this capability beyond the initial execution. These strategic extensions vary broadly and will be discussed at greater length in chapter 10. The specific ROI implications, sizable in all cases, vary as well.

For now, ponder this: Suppose you could engage your customer and vendors in systematically changing their behavior, or suppose you could improve your sales performance by motivating consistently superior selling behavior across your sales force, or suppose you could execute quickly and consistently *any* new strategic change in your company. What would that be worth to you?

BEYOND FINANCIAL RETURN

So far, we have focused on behavioral leadership's proven link to financial impact. Yet this is only part of the story. Additional benefits follow when leaders focus on motivating employees' *discretionary performance* of new behavior (discretionary performance is their highly engaged, "want to do" performance). Though less tangible, these benefits are at least as important strategically and emotionally:

- **The Culture Benefit: Improved work culture that engages employees and retains top talent.** As we mentioned in the health-care insurer's experience, employee engagement moved from "worst to first." In the Kurrizzo plant example, the employee commitment index jumped 70 percent within the year. Chapter 8 describes in more detail how some behavioral leaders are intentionally transforming culture as a competitive advantage.

- **The Change Execution Benefit: Accelerated deployment of strategic changes (via superior execution capability).** We'll discuss this more in chapter 7, but the health-care insurer we've profiled here offers one of many examples. Eighteen months after its initial work to develop and leverage behavioral leadership capability, the leadership announced a business model transformation that posed very difficult challenges, including technology and process change, structural change, and significant job reductions. Post-implementation, senior management concluded that the behavioral leadership approaches led to one of the smoothest, fastest, and most successful initiatives of that kind that had ever been undertaken.

- **The Shared Capability Benefit: Measurable proficiency in behavioral leadership skills common across leaders and managers.** The ability to measure who has attained proficiency across a group of managers and who has not enables senior leaders to steer the very progress they seek. Meanwhile, possessing such skills in unison yields far greater results than sporadic skillfulness.

- **The Personal Benefit: Emotional reward from achieving new results and making a positive difference in people's work lives.** As one manager from the company cited earlier relates, "There are too many positive impacts to name. I am old school, with seventeen years in the army. Yet, [behavioral leadership] changed my life.

What more can I say?" Another manager agrees. "You can only kick butt so much. What do you do afterwards? People get calluses and they understand—they know how to figure out the game. But, inspiring people, that's really what this process is all about."

. . .

Behavioral leadership produces stunning results, as our data demonstrates. A full understanding of these results requires both new eyes and new math. Behavioral leaders deploy the cost of leadership neglect and other new quantitative measures to estimate ROI potential and to determine where, when, and how long to invest in behavioral capability.

Math is one thing, but unlocking vast amounts of new value in an organization using behavioral leadership only happens with determined and skillful application of behavioral knowledge itself. We'll provide the essentials of this knowledge in the next chapter. Then we'll showcase actual leading-edge companies that are already applying behavioral leadership to address their most pressing tasks, challenges, and processes.

➲ THE BEHAVIORAL LEADER'S SNAPSHOT SUMMARY

In brief:

- Strong evidence exists that behavioral leadership methods consistently drive targeted behavior change, which then leads to significant results improvement.

- The Behavior → Results connection has been demonstrated for a wide spectrum of performance areas, including revenue growth, cost management, customer satisfaction, safety, cycle-time reduction, environmental compliance, and reliability (among others).

- This evidence comes from scores of organizational applications across several industries over the last two decades and is verified by the firsthand experience of these companies as well as rigorous data analysis that confirms these conclusions.

- Return on investment for building behavioral leadership capability typically ranges from five to thirty times within twelve to twenty-four months.

- Behavioral leadership introduces a "new math" that quantifies the cost of leadership neglect, the cost of partial adoption, the value of sustainability, and the value of capability extensions in subsequent implementation cycles.

- Nonfinancial benefits that companies routinely achieve include improved culture and employee engagement, accelerated change deployment, shared leadership capability, and personal fulfillment from making a positive difference in people's work lives.

Ask yourself:

☐ Do we measure the impact of behavior change on results impact, with an eye toward improving this linkage over time?

☐ Do we invest in building behavior change skills?

☐ Do we measure the return on this investment?

CHAPTER THREE

➲ DRIVERS OF SUSTAINABLE HIGH PERFORMANCE

Laura Methot, Jim Hillgren, Steve Jacobs, Danielle Geissler, Bridget Russell, and Charles Carnes

The whole of science is nothing more than a refinement of everyday thinking.
— ALBERT EINSTEIN

How do you embed the right new behaviors into an organization so you can quickly get the right new results and sustain them over a long period? Behavioral leaders do a number of things, including working behavior into annual business plan deployment, investing resources into building a high-performance culture, and enabling managers to provide high-performance coaching throughout an organization.

Yet before embarking on any of this, leaders must first understand the foundations upon which lasting behavior change rests. The science behind behavioral leadership is logical and practical, and the principles are easy to grasp—in fact, some will seem like common sense, and you may wonder why everyone isn't using them. We will look at a very rich leadership tool kit, providing models and guidelines that build on decades of rigorous scientific study.

THE BEHAVIORAL LEADERSHIP TOOL KIT

I. DCOM: The four cornerstones of sustainable high performance

II. Your range of levers

- Traditional organizational levers
- Powerful leadership levers

III. Applied Behavioral Science: Your *real* leverage

- ABCs of Applied Behavioral Science
- Pinpointing behaviors
- E-TIP Analysis for understanding and managing consequences
- Pyramid of Consequences

We begin by presenting the powerful DCOM® Model for sustainable high performance in organizations.

I. DCOM: THE FOUR CORNERSTONES OF SUSTAINABLE HIGH PERFORMANCE

The CEO of a major commodities company asked a task force of thirty leaders of global organizations and two of our colleagues to determine how companies in any industry achieve sustainable top-quartile total shareholder return. They were given six months to find a solution. Initially, task force members considered technology and hard assets (e.g., implementing new manufacturing methods or acquiring long-term rights to raw materials), but they found that these factors didn't differentiate high performers for very long.

What *did* distinguish high-performing companies—for a period of ten years or more—was their approach to *making the company better as an organization*—in other words, the company's culture and the behaviors underlying it.

Analyzing volumes of data in many industries, the team arrived at four elements of culture that in turn yielded a model for delivering sustained high performance. These four elements—the cornerstones of high performance—were Direction, Competence, Opportunity, and Motivation, shorthanded as DCOM.[1] These elements corresponded, respectively, to four distinct questions:

- Does everyone in the company clearly understand what is most important? (the Direction)

- Are the organization and its people able to achieve what is important? (their Competence)

- Are all needed resources available, and is the organization removing barriers to performance? (the Opportunity)

- Do the consequences for people's daily actions clearly align with the Direction to inspire desired behaviors? (the Motivation)

The company's CEO dismissed this model and the evidence underlying it—not once but twice—thinking it inconceivable that something as vague as culture and behavior could impact business performance. On the third attempt, the task force leader offered the findings in one hand and task force members' resignations in the other, imploring the CEO to take the research seriously.

Once he understood the data that the team had collected and the logic of its conclusions, the CEO accepted the model's validity and directed the company to implement widespread organizational changes. The CEO himself requested executive coaching and engaged us to coach ten of his top people. We worked with teams throughout the company to reengineer behavior—and through it, culture—from top to bottom. As we completed the transformation, the company for the first time in its history claimed a place in the top quartile of shareholder return.

In the years since, this company has continued to ascend the ranks of Fortune 50 companies. Meanwhile, we have deployed this model at large corporations in diverse industries: electronics, defense, chemicals, transportation, finance, insurance, health care, parcel delivery, manufacturing, pharmaceuticals, and so on. Again and again, the four cornerstones have guided leaders in designing organizational infrastructure that produces sustained high performance.

Do the DCOM cornerstones seem obvious? Closer analysis reveals that they are not. Let's look at each element more closely. As you read, keep your own company in mind. Many leaders who discover DCOM are startled to recognize themselves and their organizations in the model, for better or for worse.

Cornerstone 1: Direction

Does everyone understand the priorities? To effect behavior change, leaders must articulate three things especially well: vision, values, and value-oriented metrics.

Vision. In our research, sustained high-performance companies articulated a clear sense of purpose. Organizations gave this different names— "vision," "mission," and so on—but at high-performing companies, *all employees knew the purpose and understood how their job supported it.* At mediocre companies, employees understood their job but not how it fit into the purpose. Companies communicated their plans and objectives for the year without saying much about the organization's goals. Since most employees seek reasons to take pride in what they do, mediocre companies found it difficult to excel in the absence of a higher collective meaning.

Values. Articulating a purpose wasn't enough. High-performing organizations published their values as well, and beyond that, they took four additional actions:

- They *behaviorized* their values, describing in plain language what people actually do to realize them, day in and day out (e.g., "Ask people for their input," "Acknowledge people's past contributions," "Insist that conversations about a person involve them directly").

- They had leaders at all levels *model behaviors* consistent with values, recognizing that employees tended to scrutinize leaders' behavior in shaping their own.

- They had leaders *watch for and applaud employee actions consistent with company values*, and in general establish feedback mechanisms that helped employees understand how well they were living those values.

- Finally, they *evaluated all decisions and actions against the values*, publicly owning up to instances when actions and values didn't align.

Value-oriented metrics. High-performing companies have metrics that demonstrate customer-value delivery. In underperforming companies, traditional financial and productivity metrics induced dysfunctional behaviors, reinforced silos, and created performance barriers. Some companies espoused customer-first strategies but then undermined them by letting departmental metrics for productivity and cost control drive decisions. High-performing companies, by contrast, embraced customer-oriented metrics that reflected delivery of genuine value. These metrics encouraged *collaborative behaviors* rather than traditional egocentric, competitive behaviors that impeded performance.

As we discovered, *how* leaders went about establishing direction mattered very much. Executives at the best companies communicated only one to three clear priorities; at mediocre-performing companies, ten or more initiatives diluted executives' own time, energy, and resources. Also, leaders at high-performing companies showed constancy of purpose, disciplining themselves to stay the course. At underperforming companies, wavering signaled to employees that an initiative was just another "flavor of the month" to which the leader was paying lip service.

Cornerstone 2: Competence

Are the organization and its people capable of achieving its vision and purpose? Competence includes several kinds of capabilities and competencies.

Technical capability most often jumps to mind when people hear the word "competence." It includes functional knowledge and the skills necessary to perform the organization's tasks: engineering, marketing, accounting principles, human resource practices, software skills. Both conventionally performing and high-performing companies in our research prioritized technical capability, but other kinds of competencies proved just as critical, and only the high-performing companies consistently prioritized these.

For instance, take **collaboration skills**. At high-performing companies, leaders promoted collaboration through selection, training, and practice. But collaboration meant more than just cooperation; it meant mutual support and shared success. Most mediocre companies purposely or inadvertently promoted a competitive environment, which impeded collaboration.

Work-management skills likewise distinguished high-performing companies from mediocre ones. As our research found, employees worked most effectively when equipped with work-management skills such as decision making, problem solving, prioritizing work flow, and so on.

Finally, high-performing organizations taught **economic literacy** to employees, ensuring that people understood how the organization made money and providing employees with pathways to better operating efficiency and value creation. The vast majority of companies that we studied neglected economic literacy, assuming that employees didn't care about the organization's economics and wouldn't understand anyway. That was far from the truth. As high-performing companies learned, employees craved this information, and once they had it, they used it.

Cornerstone 3: Opportunity

Are all needed resources available, and is the organization removing barriers to performance? Employees often work extra hard to succeed through a difficult period or to achieve new performance goals, yet the company might discourage this desired behavior if it does not give employees what they need to take action. The research found that creating an environment where employees had the opportunity to excel involved four things:

- **Sufficient authority to perform their jobs well.** At mediocre companies, employees were best equipped to make decisions regarding their work, but the organization overmanaged them and located decision-making power up the hierarchy.

- **Clear and consistent boundaries.** At high-performing companies, employees understood limits to their behavior, but they also knew where they could take liberties to deliver on the organization's value proposition.

- **Proper work processes to facilitate performance.** High-performing companies also refined these processes until they ran smoothly, giving work teams authority to make improvements. In conventional organizations, employees followed processes as management demanded, even when they knew some tasks were not adding value.

- **All resources needed to get the job done well.** These included time, information, people, physical locations, money, materials, tools, and technologies.

Only by attending to all four of these dimensions did organizations systematically remove obstacles and achieve high performance.

Cornerstone 4: Motivation

Do the consequences that employees experience for their daily actions clearly align with the Direction to inspire desired behaviors?

High-performing organizations *helped people feel good about doing a good job.* They enabled people to understand the day-to-day activities needed to get the job done and provided frequent, candid feedback. Most important, they confirmed that people felt appreciated, establishing consistent and appropriate rewards for the right behavior and effective and constructive remedies for undesired behavior. In fact, employees in these companies reported a **4:1 ratio of positive to constructive feedback**. By comparison, employees in conventionally performing companies reported a 1:20 ratio.

Behavioral science holds that encouraging or discouraging consequences that follow a behavior determine whether an individual will repeat the behavior. To sustain high motivation, high-performing organizations we studied delivered consequences using **real-time, data-based feedback**, creating an environment that motivated "want to do" or **discretionary performance** as opposed to "have to do," compliant performance.

In addition, the **consequences for behavior aligned fully with direction**; not only did companies make the alignment explicit to employees ("Your emails reflect our vision of putting the customer first by offering help"), but also all consequences were aligned (e.g., adjusting call-handling productivity targets and performance feedback to be consistent with the "customer first" priority).

Finally, high-performing companies **aligned formal and informal systems for delivering consequences**. Again, much of this might sound like common sense, but too often individuals and organizations discourage people from doing the right thing and applaud people for doing the wrong thing. To perform at their best, companies cannot leave performance feedback and consequences to chance. Rather, they must design processes and practices to deliver the right consequences for the right behavior and results.

II. YOUR RANGE OF LEVERS

We have described the four cornerstones for sustainable high performance, but we haven't yet addressed the range of levers behavioral leaders utilize, nor have we discussed the principles for determining which levers provide the most power in a given set of circumstances.

Most leaders steer companies by falling back on a small set of **organizational levers** like new policies, structures, or compensation designs. Behavioral leaders see it differently: They operate with a shared *range of levers* and with a commonly understood logic for how best to ensure the necessary Direction, Competence, Opportunity, and Motivation for sustained high performance.

Behavioral leaders also apply behavioral insights to determine which of the broader set of levers—organizational processes and leadership practices—supplies the *real* leverage in a given situation. By applying an understanding of how and why people behave, behavioral leaders can greatly increase the power and sustainability of their decisions, producing the kinds of results that, as we've seen, can only be described as revolutionary.

Organizational Levers Alone May Not Get You There

A brief anecdote evokes the problems many executives have with levers. The president of a life insurance company and his executive team wanted to clarify their strategy for growth through acquisitions. The group began by reviewing first-quarter performance. It was mid-April, organic growth numbers were just available, and they were seeing them for the first time.

Piecing together various reports and perspectives, members of the team found themselves falling short of their 15 percent organic growth target. First-quarter sales lingered 3 percent above the prior year's, and the end-of-year outlook appeared to be no more than 5 percent growth.

A few senior leaders argued for replacing one-third to one-half of the sales force. Others countered that managers should focus on remedying a flawed sales-compensation plan. A third group held that the company really needed new metrics that would enable the senior team to see these things coming.

Here were intelligent, committed leaders who knew their business and respected one another, yet they made three very different assumptions about the causes of the problem they faced. Let's apply the four DCOM cornerstones to understand.

The leaders who supported hiring new sales reps believed that the current sales force lacked the necessary *Competence* for their line of business, and they assumed that hiring new people would best enable the company to gain the needed skills. Those who supported changes in sales compensation believed "you get what you pay for" and that the sales force lacked sufficient *Motivation* to "shoot the lights out."

The contingent endorsing new management metrics honed in on the senior team's lack of *Opportunity* to take more immediate action and assumed that an improved management information system (MIS) would address this. And everyone took the *Direction* for granted, making no mention of this cornerstone.

As a group, this team lacked at least two things: an explicit set of organizational levers that they could consider systematically, and a way to articulate simply and clearly the assumptions that they were making about the underlying cause of the performance challenge.

Let's tackle the first of these problems, using the DCOM Model. The organizational levers in Figure 3 are a useful starting point for senior teams.

We have derived this set of organizational levers from decades of work in the field of *whole systems architecture*. Senior teams can tailor it to their unique circumstances, adding or deleting levers or changing the terminology. What matters most is that senior teams share an explicit set of organizational levers that lists a full range of elements, linking them to the DCOM cornerstones of sustainable high performance.

ORGANIZATIONAL LEVERS	
Direction	• Mission/purpose • Values • Strategy • Goals and metrics • Communication processes

Competence	• People systems
	  ○ Career development
	  ○ Recruitment and selection
	  ○ Strategic talent management
	  ○ Onboarding and assimilation
	  ○ Training
	  ○ Performance management
	  ○ Exiting
	• Information and measurement

Opportunity	• Technology • Facilities • Core work processes • Decision-making • Structure and roles
Motivation	• Performance management (formal) • Recognition • Reward

Figure 3. Organizational leves that support the DCOM cornerstones

The Power of Leadership Levers

Although the list of organizational levers is lengthy, it does not represent the full range of levers—or even the strongest ones—available to a leadership team. Leaders' day-to-day practices can complement these organizational levers and in fact may confer even greater power. Because such practices afford a distinct and additional source of leverage, we call them

leadership levers. Examples of such leadership levers include communicating how team goals link to serving customers and supporting colleagues in other areas, clarifying high-impact behaviors for key performer groups, demonstrating a 4:1 ratio of positive to constructive feedback, and so on.

Let's return to the life insurance company's senior team. The group agreed to two steps. First, they would listen to really understand one another's point of view. Second, they would list a more complete set of organizational alternatives at their disposal and consider these as well.

They agreed that turning over the field sales force felt decisive and would send a clear message, but the disruption to the survivors would likely impede, not propel, sales performance. In fact, they had already churned nearly 60 percent of the field force with a new hiring model the prior year.

They did note that market-specific selling skills might require some attention. They also acknowledged the need for metrics but agreed that these would not fix the problem at hand.

That left the option of sales-compensation redesign. But given business travel and spring vacation, the design team wouldn't be chartered for a few weeks, until early May. The company wouldn't approve the redesign until August. With a September rollout, the company would, at best, see impact only for the last three months of the year.

By focusing on the compensation redesign lever in this way, the senior team would gain precious little leverage for closing the current year's performance gap!

At this point, the leadership team turned to leadership levers. One team member admitted, "Frankly, I haven't gone there because I'm not sure what this would really look like." With others concurring, the group asked some questions:

- Out of the thirty-three field office managers, do we feel that some consistently outperformed others? ("Absolutely.")

- Did this differential performance owe to differences in access to corporate processes and systems? ("Certainly not.")

- Did this differential performance owe to differences in the regional markets? ("To some extent, but this is not the main driver. You could put some of our field office managers in any office in the system and they would outperform the rest.")

- So some field office managers outperform others because of what they are *doing,* is this correct? ("Yes, if you put it that way.")

- Whatever they are doing differently, let's call these "leadership practices" (i.e., your leadership levers). If all field office managers were demonstrating these leadership practices consistently, would sales performance increase across the system? ("It is highly likely.")

- If we pull the top field office managers together, along with some of the top salespeople, could we identify the high-impact seller behaviors and field office manager leadership practices by the end of April? ("We've never done this before, but it's feasible.")

- Once identified, can we begin to focus all thirty-three field office managers on the same set of leadership practices, including their role in motivating consistent high-impact seller behaviors, in the month of May? ("Yes, if we get moving now.")

The senior team concluded that leadership practices—leadership levers—would enable them to implement improvements much more quickly, more than doubling the window that year when improvements would come into effect, leaving the company with the consistent selling behavior it needed.

The team also discerned a clear downside: They had not done this before, so they feared failure. What if people didn't change behavior quickly or consistently enough?

Discomfort notwithstanding, the group pulled the leadership lever. They completed their April and May milestones as planned, developed approaches for encouraging seller behavior and field office manager practices, and came very close to achieving their 15 percent organic growth target for the year.

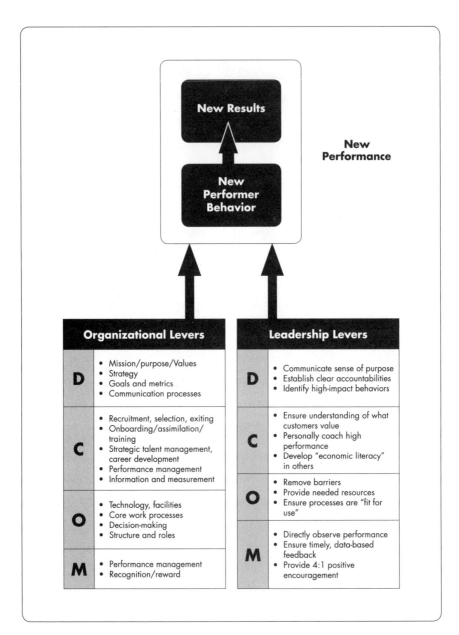

Figure 4. The performance levers model that behavioral leaders use to evaluate their options

Figure 4 illustrates the performance-levers decision tool that behavioral leaders use to evaluate their range of levers, as the insurance company leadership team did in this example.

As they weigh alternatives for encouraging new performance, behavioral leaders go one step further. They not only consider which drivers will prompt the right new behavior, but they also consider those that will sustain highly motivated behavior change. This is where their knowledge of Applied Behavioral Science provides unparalleled advantage.

III. APPLIED BEHAVIORAL SCIENCE: YOUR *REAL* LEVERAGE

As we see with levers, the four cornerstones are only a starting point to superior performance. But we're not done yet. It is possible to derive additional advantage by probing deeper into some of the cornerstones. Applied Behavioral Science (ABS) takes the understanding of one cornerstone, Motivation, to a much higher level. ABS provides a turbocharger for behavior change that leads to superior execution and sustained high performance.

Behavioral scientists have long studied how best to influence behavior. Decades of research have yielded answers, and behavioral scientists and consultants have translated these answers into organizational management methods that work in real, complex (and sometimes very large) organizations. Applying these methods, leaders can understand why they're getting current behaviors, and they can determine what alternative behavior they need instead. We begin by examining a fundamental model called *ABC,* which behavioral leaders can use to trigger and sustain new behavior to obtain desired results.

The ABCs of Applied Behavioral Science

Validated by countless scientific studies, the **ABC model** captures the process by which all behaviors take place. We define a *behavior* as what we do

would put the leader in a far better position to help crews complete their jobs effectively.

The 80/20 Paradox: What Matters Most Gets the Least Attention

After pinpointing high-impact behaviors, managers must understand what drives these behaviors *from the performer's perspective* (since this is the only perspective that has any influence on performers). ABC analysis provides a snapshot of behavior and its surrounding antecedents and consequences that lets us see clearly why certain behaviors do or don't occur. ABC also helps us identify strategies for encouraging desired behaviors and discouraging undesired behaviors.

Antecedents and consequences are quite unequal in their impact. Antecedents typically get a lot of attention—after all, they are the things that get a new behavior started—but they frequently fail to have lasting impact. *Consequences are much more important for sustained behavior change—yet are often ignored.* If you want to stop smoking, it's not enough to resolve to quit and throw out your cigarettes—those are just antecedents, with little influence per se. You also need to create strong consequences that encourage you to stop smoking. In practice, that might mean no longer hanging out with smoking buddies, and instead associating with nonsmokers who quickly complain if you light up. As addiction counselors will tell you, such social pressure constitutes a very powerful consequence in the ABC analysis of smoking. Or it could mean rewarding yourself for quitting—say, by putting aside the money you've saved each day in a glass container so that you can see the progress you are making toward taking the Alaskan cruise vacation that you've longed for.

At work, leaders who find that workers are taking shortcuts and not following standard operating procedures may send them to training—which is a well-meaning and traditional antecedent to get desired behavior. Yet training often disappoints, because workers go back to the same environment where the consequences for taking shortcuts are highly encouraging ("It's easier to do," "It takes less time," "We get recognized for completing our work quickly and punished if we're too slow") and those for following procedures are discouraging ("Doing it the prescribed way takes more time and is harder").

You can be sure that if a behavior happens consistently over time, there are *encouraging consequences that reliably follow it.* (Think of your own personal habits, good or poor.) Conversely, when a desired behavior doesn't exist, the right consequences will likely prove to be missing in action.

In general, *antecedents used alone exert only about 20 percent of the influence over behavior (antecedents get behavior started), but consequences hold the most power, about 80 percent, in sustaining behavior over time.* And further, antecedents quickly lose their power to prompt behavior if they do not pair with the right kinds of consequences.

In the business world, here's the problem: Most organizations invest 80 percent of their time, budget, and attention on getting things started (project plans, communications, training, etc.)—in other words, on the antecedents that have only 20 percent influence on behavior change. They invest much less on setting up truly effective consequences to strongly encourage sustained behavior change. Thus they fall prey to what we call the 80/20 Paradox.

Returning to the physician hand-washing example, countless hospitals have implemented a range of solutions for bolstering consistency, including slogans, admonishing signs, strategically placed gel dispensers, free movie tickets for departments with the best compliance, and even reminders that the Hippocratic oath requires them to prevent harm, which could include washing one's hands. Viewed through the ABC lens, most of these well-meaning attempts to change behavior are indeed antecedents. And hand-washing compliance rates are typically only one-third to two-thirds of what they need to be, a repeated finding that is both perplexing and unnerving. From an Applied Behavioral Science perspective, it's a good bet that the balance of consequences for doctors is the key to understanding, and overcoming, this challenge. After all, all behavior is rational, *if* you understand the drivers. Let's take a further look.

E-TIP Analysis of Consequences: A Power Tool for Behavioral Leaders

Consequences can either encourage or discourage behavior, but science has shown that not all encouraging and discouraging consequences are created equal. Some have *way* more influence, depending on the individual. As a leader, you need to assess which of the many possible consequences will most influence behavior, and conduct this analysis from the point of view of individual workers.

An especially powerful tool in this regard is *E-TIP*. The **E** in E-TIP stands for **E**ffect: Will a consequence *encourage* or *discourage* future behavior? The **TIP** stands for **T**iming, **I**mportance, and **P**robability. To determine which consequences are going to have the most influence, ask three questions:

- **Timing (Timely or Delayed?).** Does the person performing the behavior experience the consequence *immediately* or soon after the behavior, or is it significantly *delayed?*

- **Importance (Important or relatively Unimportant?).** Does the person performing the behavior care a lot or a little about the consequence?

- **Probability (Probable or Unlikely?).** In the performer's view, is the consequence highly likely to happen, or unlikely to occur?

Ample research and daily experience both confirm: Consequences that happen sooner rather than later, that the performer regards as important, and that are highly likely influence behaviors most powerfully over time.

Let's look at what happens from the hospital doctors' perspective by performing an E-TIP Analysis® (Figure 6). Knowledge, caring, enabling equipment, and well-intended programs notwithstanding, doctors experience a mix of consequences that are misaligned with the desired behavior. Hand washing takes precious time away from patient contact, at times further delaying doctors who are already running late for their scheduled rounds. Constant hand washing is tedious and often creates skin

| A → B ↔ C | | | Consequence Analysis (E-TIP) | | | |
Antecedents	Behavior	Consequences	EFFECT on behavior (Encourage, Discourage)	TIMING (Timely, Delayed)	IMPORTANCE to performer (Important, Unimportant)	PROBABILITY (Probable, Unlikely)
• "Wash hands" signs • Alcohol-based gel dispensers handy • Hippocratic oath: prevent harm • Understand bacterial risk • Patient schedule (~20 per hour) • Belief about personal compliance rate	• Wash hands before & after all patient contact: ○ Remove rings, jewelry ○ Apply gel, enough to need 30 secs to dry ○ Rub hands & fingers, coating entire surface	Takes time away from patient interaction (1/3 of scheduled allocation)	**D**iscourager	**T**imely	**I**mportant	**P**robable
		Running late; makes me even later	**D**iscourager	**T**imely	**I**mportant	**P**robable
		Tedious repetition	**D**iscourager	**T**imely	**I**mportant	**P**robable
		Patient extends hand to shake; rude to ignore	**D**iscourager	**T**imely	**I**mportant	**P**robable
		Irritates my skin	**D**iscourager	**D**elayed	**I**mportant	**P**robable
		May prevent patient infection	**E**ncourager	**D**elayed	**I**mportant	**U**nlikely

Figure 6. E-TIP Analysis reveals consequences that mostly discourage hospital doctors from washing their hands. The darker table cells highlight these discouraging consequences; the lighter cells show only one encouraging consequence—and it is delayed and unlikely, so it has little strength.

irritation, which can, paradoxically, harbor bacteria and increase potential contagion. Sometimes patients immediately extend their hand to greet the doctor, and it feels rude not to return the gesture. And so on.

When we consider each consequence through the eyes of the doctors, we see that there are more things that discourage consistent compliance than encourage it. Even more telling, the most powerful consequences—that is, the ones that are Timely, Important, and highly Probable—are all Discouragers. When examined through the ABC/E-TIP lens, a dilemma that appeared to make no sense at all now seems perfectly sensible. Unless this balance of consequences is effectively altered, the doctors' good intentions to cleanse their hands 100 percent of the time will remain just that: good intentions that fall significantly short of goal.

In addition to creating better understanding, the ABC model can help to guide more effective action as well. Continuing our example, even though antecedents generally have less influence on behavior change than do consequences, it is still worthwhile to consider how to strengthen antecedents. One notable instance was undertaken at Cedars-Sinai Medical Center in Los Angeles. The hospital epidemiologist distributed petri dishes to each physician at a key meeting, and asked each to press his or her palm against the agar, a spongy medium designed to grow bacteria. In a few days the results were in. On each petri dish was the discernible palm print upon which large, globular masses of bacteria colonies had formed. These grotesque handprints were then photographed. One that was deemed particularly offensive was converted into a screen saver and appeared on every computer in the hospital. This simple action served as a vivid reminder to physicians that they too were carriers of disease-causing bacteria. It wasn't just *other* hospital staffers that were to blame.

Realigning the balance of consequences is, of course, particularly important to consider. Some hospitals have worked diligently to weaken the hand-washing discouragers. For instance, they have provided more time per patient in scheduled rounds and have changed the placement of gel dispensers to increase immediate access and convenience. Also, some approaches have focused on increasing the number and influence of encouragers that promote the right behavior. Examples include "Hand Hygiene Safety Posses" that roam the hospital, distributing $10 coffee gift cards to any physician caught washing his or her hands, and even prompting patients and nurses to thank doctors when they do so. And, certain institutions have also sought to strengthen the discouragers for *noncompliant* behavior. Knowing that most doctors overestimate their rate of personal compliance (often substantially), individualized hygiene report cards provide objective, individualized data to dispel erroneous beliefs.

One hospital in Pittsburgh went further and did the unthinkable: Nurses began to remind doctors on the spot if they forgot to follow the prescribed hand-washing procedure!

Regardless of the specific interventions, the general point remains: When the hospitals took specific action to realign the balance of consequences for desired and undesired behavior, improved results typically followed. *And a similar pattern holds in a workplace context for any behavior a manager might seek to encourage.*

One final note: E-TIP suggests that leaders should only consider how a consequence impacts behavior, not whether the consequence will feel good or bad. But the best leaders know that, while they may intend to provide encouraging or discouraging consequences, their intent matters far less than the *actual impact* on behaviors. These leaders don't fall into the trap of thinking, "I made sure that there were encouraging consequences for the things I was asking people to do, but they still didn't do them!" In behavioral terms, if the behavior changes, then the leader's actions were sufficiently encouraging after all.

The Art of Applying the Science

The tools that influence behavior (ABCs, E-TIP) derive from scientifically validated laws describing why we do what we do. But applying them involves more than science—it's art as well—so *behavioral leaders apply behavioral science with creativity and experienced judgment.*

Artfulness becomes relevant because "encouraging consequences" vary wildly across individuals and cultures. Here's an example. The new American leader of a Singapore plant asked a native frontline supervisor to stand for applause, hoping to reinforce his desired behavior. In Western culture, public recognition means high praise, but Singapore's collectivist culture values group harmony above individual accomplishment—so publicly recognizing personal accomplishment jeopardizes the group. The well-meaning leader's praise backfired, causing the Singaporean's fellow employees to think, "I'm not going to do what my coworker did if I'm going to be publicly revealed for it!"

Behavioral leaders also role-model desired behavior. A manufacturing plant's maintenance division had improved safety dramatically by applying the ABCs and E-TIP. They saw safety incidents decrease well below historical levels. Managers relentlessly pursued "zero" as their safety goal, wanting all workers to complete their work safely every day, but they weren't quite there. As division managers met to find their way to that elusive zero, one exclaimed, "Wait a minute! We're the ones who provide the ultimate antecedents and consequences to our people. So before we'll get anyone else to hit zero, *we* need to change first!"

That unlocked their behavioral puzzle. Division managers tried new antecedents and consequences to drive to zero, agreeing on how they would give encouraging consequences to motivate the highest safety performance and discouraging consequences to extinguish risk-taking behaviors. They would also coach their local managers on how to do so.

Soon the plant boasted only three minor injuries and no serious ones, a major accomplishment considering that three thousand new contract workers were working on-site 24/7 over forty days. That's over one million hours of work in a tough environment, performed safely.

Shaping Behavior Change

It's one thing to learn about ABS tools, and quite another to develop practical fluency in using them. Most behavioral leaders accept that they have started an ongoing process of discovery and development, understanding that they might not realize the cumulative impact for weeks or months. Behavioral leaders manage the process by creating *shaping plans* that delineate steps along the behavior change path. Behavioral leaders make sure that they can observe new steps in the right direction and reinforce these even before achieving the end goal.

Such a practice might seem like coddling, but guess what? It works!

A BEHAVIORAL LEADER SPEAKS

JOHN KEALEY, FORMER CEO, iDIRECT*

In 2001, I walked into a disaster. It looked good from the outside: a startup with game-changing technology, promising contracts, and a strong balance sheet—or so I was told. But as the new CEO, I discovered creditor complaints, issued checks that sat until funds arrived, unworkable contracts, nonpayments on obligations, and little cash.

If ever there were a need for skillful leadership, it was here. My Applied Behavioral Science training told me to start by focusing objectively and candidly on our dire condition, presenting a compelling vision for what we could become, pinpointing behaviors to execute the vision, and being transparent every step of the way.

I was painfully transparent: We had cash for two or three payrolls, and no solutions. I needed their ideas. I needed them to understand the behavioral changes needed: Spend less, finalize real opportunities, and find creative solutions.

For example, one idea helped save us early on. We subleased office space to a firm that wanted less space at lower rent. Their escrowed deposit equaled two months of payroll, and they agreed to let us use it. Those funds bought time, and we used this window to make sure that every one of us was aligned on the high-impact behavior change that would move us farthest the fastest. Traditional goals, metrics, and project plans were not sufficient. We made sure that our daily behavior drove the progress we

---

*As a result of iDirect's transformation, John was named Entrepreneur of the Year by Ernst & Young in 2005. Since then he has continued to apply his behavioral leadership acumen in successfully transitioning iDirect to a strategic global acquirer and, as CEO, leading the growth and acquisition by IBM of Vivisimo, a recognized leader in discovery and navigation software for big data. At the time of publication, John is CEO of Decision Lens.

needed—every person, every action, every day. In five years our annual revenue grew from $5 million to $120 million.

Ultimately, behavioral leadership skills made the difference. Don't make the mistake of believing that behavioral leadership is merely a nice-to-have during the good times. If you really want to maximize what's possible, it is a must-have during the toughest time.

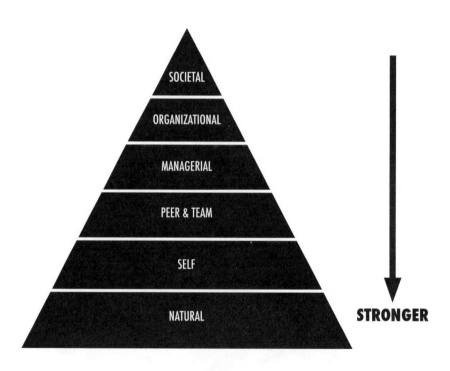

Figure 7. The Pyramid of Consequences

IMPLICATIONS FOR LEVERS AND LEVERAGE

Behavioral leadership confers an advantage in part because it explicitly deploys the underlying science to select and apply levers. We can distinguish first between levers that serve as antecedents to prompt behavior and those that function as consequences. Organizational levers that serve primarily as antecedents might not possess the power we expect.

We can also select levers based on whether they represent stronger versus weaker antecedents. For instance, high-performing organizations tend to communicate only one to three annual priorities, rather than the usual ten or more. Stated goals are indeed merely an antecedent, but clear focus strengthens their impact.

Finally, we can determine which levers serve as consequences that encourage or discourage behavior that matters. True to E-TIP, senior leaders should choose levers that employees regard as **T**imely, **I**mportant, and highly **P**robable. Well-aligned TIPs provide the *real* leverage, which is why leaders should choose organizational levers (which often are *not* timely, important, and probable) carefully along with other alternatives.

Pyramid of Consequences

Sometimes the best levers to pull are neither organizational levers nor leadership practices. ABS helps us here, too. While managing the process of behavioral change, strong behavioral leaders monitor feedback from multiple sources, and they use the **Pyramid of Consequences** to fine-tune their approaches (Figure 7). In the pyramid, the strongest consequences reside at the bottom, the weakest toward the top—which helps explain everything from why you can't change personal habits easily to why people drive too fast.

We can generate consequences from many sources—from the task itself, from oneself, from peers, from managers, and so on. The Pyramid of Consequences summarizes these sources and visually depicts their relative strength. A pyramid is strongest at its base, and so are the consequences shown there, because these consequences are more **T**imely, **I**mportant, and **P**robable than consequences at the top (which tend to be more Delayed and Unlikely). Consider for a moment three of the more potent sources of consequences.

Natural consequences. The behavior of eating a favorite food carries reinforcing consequences because the taste naturally reinforces the behavior of eating. In the workplace, interacting with customers (if you happen to love interacting with others) and solving complex problems (if you love to analyze things) also carry reinforcing consequences—serving, in effect, as their own reward. Leaders can arrange positive consequences at this level by ensuring that work itself is naturally reinforcing, given the proclivities of individuals. Leaders also can arrange access to reinforcing activities for the performer as a reward for completing a desired task.

Self-consequences. The second most powerful reinforcement comes from oneself. These consequences often take the form of positive or negative self-statements (e.g., "I really made the right decision when I delayed boarding because the pilots were not here yet and the plane was too warm for customers to sit for very long without the crew"). Positive self-statements reinforce behavior because of their previous association with external reinforcing consequences, such as positive feedback from others. Leaders can encourage self-reinforcement by asking employees how well they thought they did or prompting them to arrange a fun reward for themselves after completing a key behavior or result.

Peer and team consequences. Peers and others close to the performer deliver the third most powerful source of reinforcement. Because these people maintain valued relationships with the performer, their comments and recognition strongly impact the performer's behavior and often provide reinforcement that leads to internalization of reinforcement seen at the second (self) level. Leaders can impact this level by encouraging team members to give each other feedback.

Knowing the Pyramid Helps You Align Powerful Consequences

Behavioral leaders use the Pyramid of Consequences in important ways.

First, they analyze behavior they are observing in these terms to better understand what is happening and how to respond. One plant supervisor analyzed consequences for the undesirable behavior of a senior crew member. This worker had called the water/fuel truck driver to make a delivery six miles away from the truck shop. When the driver (a junior worker) arrived, he found that the fuel call was a prank.

The supervisor understood that the senior crew member experienced multiple encouraging consequences for his behavior: immediate gratification at seeing the look on the driver's face (natural), pleasure upon remembering the story (self), and further enjoyment while sharing the joke with his fellow workers (peers). This supervisor couldn't eliminate three powerful consequences, but he could counter them by assigning the senior worker to water/fuel truck duty for a couple of shift cycles. This proved a sufficiently discouraging consequence to make the fellow think twice about repeating the behavior that got him there.

Second, behavioral leaders go beyond organizational and leadership (managerial) sources of consequences when they find it more practical and effective to do so. One of our colleagues needed to motivate hundreds of employees at a health-care insurer to use keystrokes in new software rather than their desktop mice. She could have used organizational levers such as rapid-adoption bonuses, or leadership levers such as daily supervisor walkabouts to observe behavior and provide immediate feedback. Instead, she moved down the Pyramid of Consequences and employed a form of *natural* consequence. She and her team constructed "mouse houses" out of paper clips and placed them over the desktop mouse on each employee's desk.

While humorous, the mouse houses served a serious purpose. Rather than experience the immediacy and comfort of reaching for the mouse, employees experienced a discourager. It took them longer to remove the house than it did to use the keystrokes as intended. Rather than have managers spend hours observing behavior and providing feedback (diverting time from more important coaching), supervisors just scanned the floor to ensure that the houses were in place over the mice.

• • •

This chapter has briefed you on tools of behavioral science that behavioral leaders use to achieve breakthrough results. With these tools in hand, behavioral leaders become adept at encouraging new desired behavior and discouraging current unwanted behavior. But such skillfulness doesn't come overnight. It takes intention and practice. Through trial and error, behavioral leaders learn to improve the speed, consistency, and stickiness of behavior change. They do so by building in more powerful antecedents, systematically adding consequences that encourage desired behavior, eliminating consequences that discourage desired behavior, and strengthening consequences by increasing their timeliness, importance, and probability. Having mastered these behavior basics, behavioral leaders can then turn to running their organization with new eyes.

➲ THE BEHAVIORAL LEADER'S SNAPSHOT SUMMARY

In brief:

I. The four DCOM cornerstones of sustainable high performance:

- **Direction**. Does everyone in the organization clearly understand what is most important?

- **Competence**. Do the organization and its individuals have the capability to achieve what is important?

- **Opportunity**. Are the resources available, and are barriers to performance being addressed?

- **Motivation**. Do people want to perform, or do they just have to?

There are distinct differentiators between conventional organizations and sustained high-performing organizations, as shown in the table on the next page.

II.   Your Range of Levers

- Behavioral leaders understand their range of levers for leading new performance. Among other things, they:

  o   Link their decisions to the specific results targets and high-impact behavior that they want to encourage

  o   Use a complete and shared set of organizational levers in weighing alternatives

  o   Place equal emphasis on leadership levers and organizational levers, knowing that changing day-to-day leadership practices may at times be more effective and/or less expensive than changing organizational processes

III.   Applied Behavioral Science: Your *real* leverage

- Most organizations place 80 percent of their time, attention, and budget on the things that are intended to get new behavior started, that is, on "antecedents."

- Consequences, however, follow behavior and typically have 80 percent of the influence on whether or not people will continue that behavior.

- The E-TIP tool analyzes the four elements that determine the strength of consequences and helps leaders to better understand why current behavior is occurring, and how to establish the right balance of consequences to motivate desired behavior.

- These four E-TIP elements are the degree to which a consequence is **E**ncouraging, **T**imely, **I**mportant, and **P**robable from the perspective of the performer.

DIRECTION	Conventional Organizations	Sustained High-Performing Organizations
Mission	Published; available	Known at all levels
Values	Published; available	Behavioralized and referenced
Metrics	Cost and productivity	Value delivered to the customer
Alignment	Siloed	Across levels and functions
Priorities	10 or more	1 to 3
COMPETENCE		
Technical	Highly valued	Highly valued
Work/general management	Little interest	Highly valued
Collaboration	Individual competitiveness	Highly valued
Economic literacy	No effort to teach	Highly valued
OPPORTUNITY		
Authority	Limited through policies or supervision	Appropriate freedom to act
Boundaries	Unclear	Clear
Processes	Fixed	Flexible
Resources	Artificially limited	Adequate, fluid Not bound by org. structure
MOTIVATION		
Feedback	Limited Delayed	Real-time feedback Data-based feedback
Consequences	Not aligned with **Direction** (above) Not aligned with each other Delivered 1:20 (+/-)	Aligned with **Direction** Aligned with each other Delivered 4:1 (+/-)

Ask yourself:

☐ Does our leadership team explicitly and consistently focus on building a sustainable high-performance organization?

☐ Do we deliberately address all four DCOM cornerstones (i.e., Direction, Competence, Opportunity, and Motivation)?

☐ Considering the DCOM differentiators, in what ways are we similar to top-performing companies? Conventionally performing companies?

☐ When considering our course of action to lead performance to the next level, do we use a systematic approach to understand why current results and current behaviors occur as they do? Is this approach effective?

☐ When considering changes in organizational levers, do we

    o Explicitly discuss the new results and the new behavior that we need?

    o Use a common set of levers to ensure that we are all considering our range of options?

    o Place equal consideration of leadership practices to replace or augment changes in organizational levers?

☐ Do we place most of our time, attention, and budget on getting new behavior started (i.e., the antecedents) or on encouraging sustained behavior change (i.e., the consequences)?

☐ How well do we establish the right balance of effective consequences (i.e., **T**imely, **I**mportant, **P**robable) to change high-impact behavior?

CHAPTER FOUR

➲ PUTTING BEHAVIORAL LEADERSHIP INTO PRACTICE — SEVEN ESSENTIAL STEPS

Steve Jacobs, Debbie Kramer, and Carolina Aguilera

There is, upon the whole, nothing more important in life than to find out the right point of view from which things should be looked at and judged of, and then to keep to that point.

— CARL VON CLAUSEWITZ

Now you know the core concepts underpinning behavioral leadership. But how can behavioral leaders *apply* this knowledge to achieve revolutionary results?

Upcoming chapters describe several powerful business applications of behavioral leadership that, individually and collectively, confer new competitive advantage. Yet these applications all proceed according to seven essential steps that we believe you will find exciting and applicable to your own initiatives. Whether it's retooling an organization's culture, rethinking the annual plan, or undertaking a change initiative, *how* leaders undertake these seven steps determines the form, function, and scale of the outcome, and *how well* they undertake them determines the extent of the advantage.

THE BEHAVIORAL LEADER'S SEVEN ESSENTIAL STEPS

1. Target the Business Opportunity and Desired Results

2. Pinpoint the High-Impact Behavior

3. Understand the Drivers

4. Implement the Behavior Change Plan

5. Continuously Improve Your Own Leadership Practices

6. Measure Behavior Change Progress and Impact

7. Sustain It, Improve It, Apply It to New Priorities

STEP 1: TARGET THE BUSINESS OPPORTUNITY AND DESIRED RESULTS

Jawaharlal Nehru, India's first prime minister, once observed that "action, to be effective, must be directed to clearly conceived ends." Behavioral leaders who achieve new advantage are above all skillful and selective in their aim. They focus their behavioral capability on strategic business opportunities ranging from sales growth to innovation, cost management, capital stewardship, and culture change. Then they set worthy, precise, and challenging results targets.

We all learned the importance of goal setting in Management 101. But how many of us actually do it well? This point was driven home to one of this chapter's coauthors, Steve Jacobs, during a ski lesson. Steve's ski instructor refused at first to discuss technique. Instead, he took Steve to the top of a run that they both knew was a bit beyond Steve's ability, and asked, "What's your goal?"

"To get down the slope well and safely," Steve responded.

"That's your first problem. You won't sharpen your technique if you don't sharpen your objective." He went on to focus Steve on "carving turns" rather than "getting down the slope well." In other words, Steve needed to *target his desired results* carefully and precisely.

Consider how your organization translates priorities—such as improving innovation, customer satisfaction, or employee engagement—into results targets. Are these akin to carving turns or getting down the hill? Now consider more familiar and quantitative business priorities, such as growing sales. Same question: Can the local sales manager and the individual salesperson really pinpoint high-impact sales behaviors for the coming year without knowing more specifics about the results objective? Are you sure?

STEP 2: PINPOINT THE HIGH-IMPACT BEHAVIOR

This is a big one, almost the linchpin of behavioral leadership, yet also one of the most difficult of the seven steps to weave into everyday business. As we saw in the last chapter, behavioral leaders identify and focus on high-impact behaviors that will distinctly achieve new performance. High-impact behaviors are behaviors that:

- Drive targeted results
- Are few in number
- Do not likely happen without focused, purposeful effort
- Can pull along other desired behaviors as well

Returning to the skiing example, the instructor significantly improved Steve's skiing by focusing him on a single, specific new behavior: applying pressure on the quarter-square-inch of his inside downhill boot as he carved turns. (Yes, it was *that* specific.) Though it felt a bit awkward at first, this pinpointed focus felt different from Steve's prior focus on too many other general behaviors, such as keeping his shoulders pointed down the mountain, keeping his arms away from his body, keeping hips forward, and so on.

Does skillful pinpointing in the workplace seem straightforward? You might be thinking, "No problem." Great. But remember: Pinpointing behavior *well* takes time, rigor, and experience. Behavioral leaders proceed by asking the following three questions.

Whose behavior? Once behavioral leaders clearly target new results, they identify the people—groups or individuals—whose actions most directly influence desired results. Such *performers,* as we call them, are often, but not always, frontline employees and their supervisors.

Suppose managers target halving the cycle time for new product development or 50 percent improvement in first-year yield. Who are the key performers? They may include PhD research scientists or marketing VPs. Or suppose the performance in question is the return on big-bet capital allocations. Then the key performer group is the senior team making capital stewardship decisions. Or, if reducing cost per delivery in a food distribution center is the goal, then order processors, warehouse personnel, and delivery truck drivers all become the key performers.

Precisely what behavior? With performers identified, behavioral leaders focus on specific behaviors that will really help drive targeted results. As Alexander the Great reportedly said, "Remember: We need to win at only one point on the field, so long as that point is decisive." Behavioral leaders attend especially to behaviors that are new or complex, that will likely not happen naturally at the right frequency and quality to achieve desired results, or that will likely jeopardize the targeted results if they do not occur with sufficient frequency and quality.

As we've seen, behavioral leaders also take care to describe the behavior in objective, specific language. They avoid subjective description that moves beyond the facts to include opinions, judgments, interpretations, and labels. Objective description eliminates subjectivity by using factual and neutral words and descriptors. A pinpointed behavior should be completely objective and precise so performers are 100 percent clear on what is expected of them.

To share a simple example, a doctor reviewed lab work during a checkup and told the patient, "Your cholesterol is a bit high. You're going to need to do something about it. Otherwise, I'll have to put you on meds." That was very general and not very actionable. When the patient asked him to clarify further, his reply was pinpointed and specifically actionable: "Although your high-density cholesterol is twenty milligrams per deciliter over normal (a good thing), your low-density cholesterol is forty milligrams per deciliter over target (a bad thing). Since your diet is already relatively low in cholesterol intake, you need to do two things immediately. Lose six pounds, and begin walking ten thousand steps per day. Continue this for four months, and then we will measure your cholesterol levels to assess progress." Now, *that* is pinpointing.

At CLG, we use a convenient device called the NORMS of Objectivity (NORMS for short) to describe behavior objectively. When describing behavior, we make sure that it is **N**ot an interpretation, and that it is **O**bservable, **R**eliable, **M**easurable, and **S**pecific (Figure 8).

What supporting behavior is needed? Once behavioral leaders have used NORMS to pinpoint high-impact behaviors at the performer level, they identify a few key leadership practices that will successfully support the performer's behavior change. They do the same for second-level managers using the same principle, then third-level managers, and so on.

This approach transcends the power of goal alignment alone (which in itself is hit-or-miss in most organizations) by aligning high-impact behavior at every level. Note that high-impact behaviors for managers of key

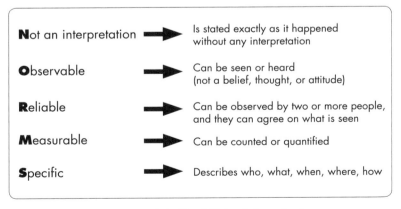

Figure 8. NORMS of Objectivity criteria

performers aren't just any leadership activities; they are **T**imely, **I**mportant, and **P**robable encouraging or discouraging practices that enable leaders to act as effective *consequence providers* (this is the "80 percent impact" we discussed in chapter 3).

Remember the health-care insurer discussed in chapter 2 that dramatically improved its customers' claims and call experience? In that situation, leaders initially convened top-performing claims processors, customer service representatives, frontline supervisors, and second-level managers to identify high-impact behaviors that, if demonstrated consistently across thousands of service personnel, would enhance the targeted results (Figure 9).

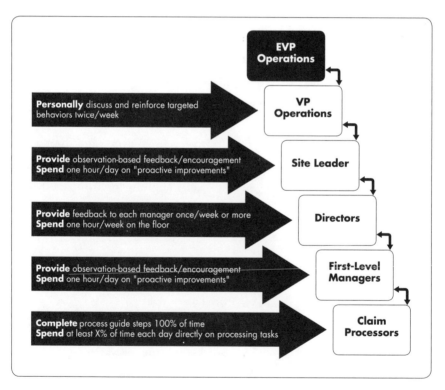

Figure 9. High-impact behavior cascade needed to improve the customer experience

For starters, a couple of high-impact behaviors were identified for claims processors, including the need to complete all steps in the process guide 100 percent of the time. Moving on to first-level managers, the group identified a number of supervisor behaviors that would help, but the group agreed that job one was observing and coaching claims-processor performance. Specifically, they agreed that the managers' first high-impact behavior was to "provide observation-based feedback/encouragement."

For directors in the service centers, the group identified "Spend one hour/week on the floor (i.e., visiting each operations area)." And so on. Even the enterprise's VP of service operations found himself on the behavior map, personally joining monthly progress reviews for each site and asking three questions: "What are you learning?" "What are you most proud of?" And "What can my team and I do to support your progress?"

 ## STEP 3: UNDERSTAND THE DRIVERS

What truly drives a behavior? Behavioral leaders can influence behavior well by analyzing its drivers. With behaviors pinpointed, behavioral leaders draw upon Applied Behavioral Science to identify the triggers (antecedents) and impact on the performers (consequences) of behavior. Figure 10 suggests the kinds of questions that help leaders understand the behavioral drivers.

If Figure 10 looks intimidating, don't worry: Sometimes a mere back-of-a-napkin analysis suffices. Other times, an enterprise requires a thorough, systematic assessment. One company spent two years and several million dollars planning and implementing the first release of a new software application. The system was well designed, released in stages so that no single release would overwhelm users, and presented with useful information about the "what and why's." Additionally, the company:

- Timed and delivered user training well

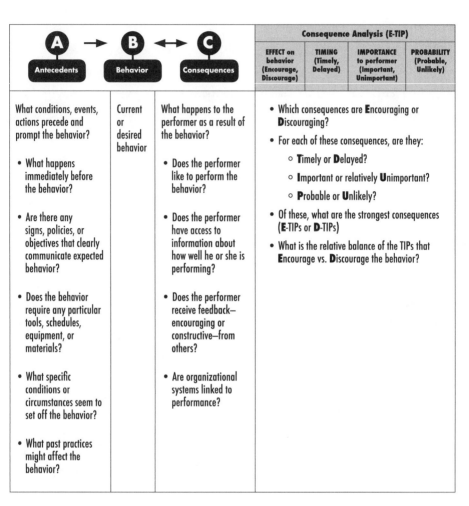

Figure 10. E-TIP Analysis of consequences helps behavioral leaders understand what drives the behavior

- Provided post-training, well-staffed help desks to field questions around the clock

- Deployed tracking systems that identified, to a person, who had and hadn't adopted the new system

- Told personnel that continuing to use the old system was not an option and that the old system would soon be phased out

But six months after the initial rollout, only 50 percent of users had adopted the new system. Project managers were exasperated. It didn't make sense. Why would half the employees continue to use an old, complex system when they had a better alternative at their fingertips (and had been asked not to use the old one)?

Was it irrational behavior? Absolutely not. *All behavior is rational—if you know the drivers.* Using an ABC analysis, we worked with project managers to identify antecedents and consequences for the desired behavior—adopting the new system—*from the users' perspective.* Listing and analyzing likely consequences, we found that a number of positive consequences for adopting the new system did exist. However, they were competing with equally powerful positive consequences for the old behavior:

- Yes, the help desk was well staffed with subject-matter experts, but employees remembered from past experience that help desks were decidedly unhelpful. The prospect of calling the help desk filled some users with a "sense of dread" or a feeling of "here we go again" (a **D**iscouraging factor that was **T**imely, **I**mportant, and in their view, **P**robable).

- Other users had a slightly more positive past experience with help desks, but only sometimes (the consequence of calling the help desk was mildly **E**ncouraging, but hard to predict or **U**nlikely).

- Even more important, employees reported receiving little positive reinforcement from managers for using the new system. When managers did deliver feedback, it was **E**ncouraging, **T**imely, and **I**mportant. However, it was also very **U**nlikely. (No feedback is still feedback, and it usually means to the user, "even though they said it's important, it's not that important.")

Longtime employees had also witnessed a number of "next big things" that fell short of expectations. In their view, it made more sense to wait and see if the new system would really prevail.

We still hadn't cracked the code entirely, so we asked: "What's keeping these folks stuck?" Managers answered: "For many of them, it's because they're losing their magic decoder rings." Their *what?* What did that mean? It turned out that employees took mastery of the old system as a badge of honor, whimsically describing it as "having a decoder ring." Seasoned employees with decoder rings were respected and enlisted as coaches. These employees reported that they had grown to *like* the complexities of the legacy system because they felt a sense of mastery (i.e., a self-consequence and powerful E-TIP). They felt they had the most to lose by migrating to the new system. They didn't like the new system, and they didn't hesitate to share their feelings.

Thanks to this analysis, the project managers came up with all kinds of creative turnaround actions. They realized they could enlist the "decoder ring masters" of the old system to become go-to subject-matter experts for the new system. They could engage frontline managers in providing daily reinforcement for adoption, as well as strong discouragers (D-TIPs) for nonadoption. And what about senior leaders? The project team could leverage them to recognize individual adopters and celebrate progress to 100 percent adoption.

Project managers would need to weigh and select their newfound alternatives carefully. But one thing was clear. Thanks to a skillful behavioral analysis and discussion, the group was excited and motivated to implement their ideas. The breakthrough had been there all along, but the team had required a different point of view to bring it to fruition.

STEP 4: IMPLEMENT THE BEHAVIOR CHANGE PLAN

As the previous example illustrates, we analyze behavior drivers so as to *do* something with this understanding: improve performance and results. Behavioral leaders never leave the actual changing of behavior to chance. They apply logical, practical, systematic techniques to develop a *behavior change plan.*

First, behavioral leaders apply effective antecedents to prompt high-impact behaviors. Three of the DCOM cornerstones discussed in chapter 3 serve as a useful guide here. Antecedents need to provide clear *Direction* regarding what specific behavior is expected. They should ensure that performers have basic *Competence* by providing training and ongoing skill development. And antecedents need to ensure people's *Opportunity* to perform the desired behavior by providing sufficient time, information, processes and tools, budget, and so on.

In the software implementation example, project leaders had incorporated important antecedents to trigger new user behavior (e.g., training and communications about what was changing and why). Project leaders also knew that the right encouragement by frontline supervisors for new adoption would prove powerful.

However, they neglected to consider *how* to get hundreds of these frontline supervisors to provide feedback and discourage use of the old system. Powerful antecedents for supervisors could have included:

- A starter set deployment plan to show each supervisor what they were expected to do and when (including how often to provide feedback)

- Skill-building mini-workshops or coaching on request to ensure supervisors felt comfortable providing feedback

- A reduction in department meetings during the rollout period to allow time for one-on-one discussions with team members

Second, behavioral leaders seek to rebalance consequences by encouraging desired behavior and discouraging undesired behavior (Figure 11).

The team members realized that 95 percent of their plans applied to frontline system users, and they had largely ignored supervisors, the most powerful influencers of behavior change. Supervisors can provide **T**imely, **I**mportant, and **P**robable encouragers and discouragers because of their proximity to the front line. So, the new plan focused on how supervisors could encourage desired behaviors and discourage undesired behaviors.

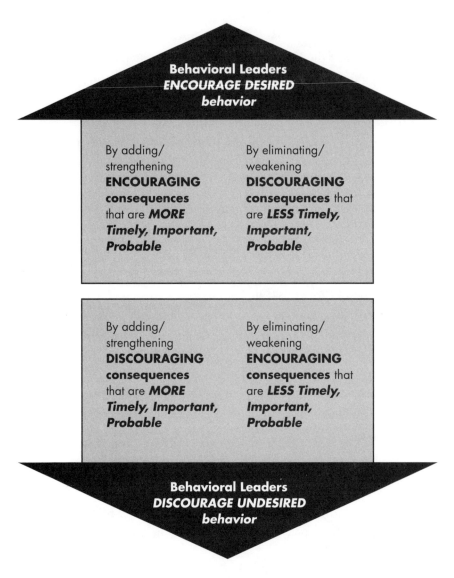

Figure 11. "TIPping" the balance of consequences in the right direction

The team added new encouraging consequences for the desired behaviors. Supervisors set adoption goals with positive consequences for adoption (e.g., time off with sales coverage if every team member opened/closed deals using the new software). Supervisors had to verify that behaviors were occurring, and they had to give positive, timely feedback when they were. They also tracked scorecard targets to celebrate the impact of using the new system and enlisted superusers to role model desired behaviors and give positive feedback.

Further, supervisors added discouraging consequences for undesired behaviors. They had to verify that behaviors were occurring and give timely, constructive feedback if they were not. They also performed behavior risk analyses to identify people who could potentially resist the change (at times redirecting many of them to actually lead the change to the new system).

A third technique that behavioral leaders use in developing and implementing behavior plans is shaping (mentioned briefly in the last chapter). Rather than waiting until they achieve a new result before reinforcing the new behavior, behavioral leaders accelerate the behavior change process by observing and reinforcing new, successive steps in the right direction.

Discretionary Performance

Behavioral leaders excel at encouraging the adoption and sustainability of desired behavior from the get-go. They focus on getting the right people doing the right things for the right reasons—leading performers to say, "I *want* to do this" (discretionary performance) versus "I *have* to do this" (compliance). In the former scenario, employees accomplish much more.

Could the company in the software implementation story have tried to *make* people adopt the new system by giving up the carrot and embracing the stick? Yes, and they might have achieved short-term compliance with negative consequences every time adoption wavered. But full yield from the new system—not to mention sustainability over time—comes from the zeal of employees who *want* to make the new system work.

Individuals who engage in compliant, "have to do" performance simply avoid the unpleasant consequences that would be delivered if performance dropped below a minimum. Without the right consequences, employees will work to stay just above that level, but not strive to go beyond. In stark contrast, the discretionary, "want to do" performance of committed employees reflects their desire to experience the fruits of extraordinary achievement. To achieve this "want to do" behavior, behavioral leaders bolster consequences that encourage desired behavior, not simply consequences that discourage undesired behavior (Figure 12).

As a senior leader, you know what must be accomplished. You might even know what people need to do to accomplish it. But that's not the issue. The real question is, 'How do I help them know what they need to do and, most importantly, want to do it?' Behavioral leadership provides the key to asking and answering this question. It has fundamentally changed the way I lead, and what we have accomplished together.

— JOHN KEALEY, CEO AND ERNST & YOUNG ENTREPRENEUR OF THE YEAR

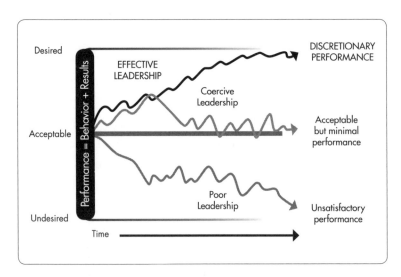

Figure 12. The important role of discretionary performance. "Leadership is the art of getting someone to do something you want done because he wants to do it." —Dwight D. Eisenhower

One final point on discretionary performance: Many companies seek to build employee engagement throughout their organizations, but behavioral leaders go further. They do this by fostering the discretionary performance of their people, usually by targeting the high-impact behaviors that directly improve business results and competitive advantage. As you'll see in chapter 8, they use the proven methods of ABS to build sustainable, high-engagement cultures.

 ## STEP 5: CONTINUOUSLY IMPROVE YOUR OWN LEADERSHIP PRACTICES

Behavioral leaders who want to change others' behavior and foster discretionary performance must be willing to change their own behavior too. This may not seem like a big deal, but how many leaders really walk the talk?

In researching their book *Beyond Performance,* transformational change expert Scott Keller and colleagues found that leaders typically don't see themselves as part of the problem.[1] Speaking behaviorally, most leaders don't understand their personal role in ensuring that the right antecedents and consequences prevail in their work environments.

Behavioral leaders not only accept that they may in fact be part of the problem, but they also see themselves as *part of the solution* in shaping new, high-impact behavior. Rather than focus on sweeping "improve my leadership" objectives, they look to adjust their personal leadership practices continually to enhance their positive impact. After all, as mentioned in the previous chapter, reshaping leadership practices often constitutes the fastest and least expensive lever for changing performer behavior.

Behavioral leaders belong in what we call Q4, the "winning quadrant" of the **Q4 Leadership model** (Figure 13). Q4 leaders get sustainable long-term results, have engaged and committed employees, and they achieve this through their leadership behaviors.

The Q4 model rests on fifty years of research and experience, from

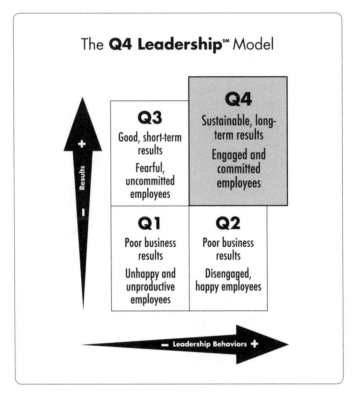

Figure 13. The Q4 Leadership model

Blake and Mouton's[2] distinction between "concern for production" and "concern for people" to Jack Welch's distinction at GE between "what" leaders accomplish and "how" they accomplish it. The Q4 model focuses on two types of leadership practices: results-driven practices and engagement-focused practices. Let's explore the model quadrant by quadrant.

Q1 leaders neither drive results nor engage employees. They do not reliably establish clear, consistent direction or provide meaningful, reinforcing feedback. They overlook ways to build employees' competence and provide opportunity for them to perform at high levels. Focusing on activity rather than outcomes, they leave employees apathetic and cynical.

Q2 leaders establish a positive work environment, removing barriers that frustrate their teams, recognizing progress individually and collectively, and showing genuine concern for their people. Still, they underemphasize performance, fail to set high standards, don't hold people accountable for reaching standards, don't provide constructive feedback, and don't act on persisting performance issues. People often enjoy working for these leaders, but they often leave behind inconsistent-performance track records.

Q3 leaders achieve results, at least in the short term. They set high standards, place a premium on selecting top talent, hold people accountable, provide negative consequences for missing objectives, and reward top performance with end-of-year bonuses. But they do not work to build discretionary performance by coaching employees over time, demonstrating genuine caring for team members, or ensuring a 4:1 ratio of positive to constructive feedback. The eventual result: Q3 leaders build temporary high performance that cannot endure beyond their reign, and they typically cannot retain high performers.

Q4 leaders are most effective over time. They not only believe that leaders can produce superior results and build high engagement; they understand that leaders must strive to achieve both together. *This is the essence of behavioral leadership: reaching new and sustainable results by motivating broad-based discretionary performance of the right new behavior.* Examples of such Q4 Leadership practices are summarized in Figure 14.

Behavioral leaders seek to sharpen Q4 practices that foster superior and sustainable results through high engagement. No matter how effective they already are, they always look to improve their own leadership behavior. They work hard to trigger the right new behavior, deploying the right balance of consequences to establish clear **D**irection, enable the right skills (**C**ompetence), provide the right enablers (**O**pportunity), and **M**otivate high engagement.

STEP 6: MEASURE BEHAVIOR CHANGE PROGRESS AND IMPACT

How many organizations or leaders today really know if behavior change happens as consistently or effectively as intended?

Direction	Competence	Opportunity	Motivation
• **Ensures our team has measurements** that are helpful and consistent with what needs to be done • **Clarifies expectations** about specific behaviors needed to achieve our goals (when appropriate) • **Communicates a sense of purpose** that makes work objectives meaningful and inspiring • **Provides specific goals** for performance	• **Demonstrates collaboration** between self and others • **Ensures that we understand how what we do adds value** to our customers • **Addresses mistakes and problems** as opportunities for learning • **Demonstrates commitment** to development of technical and work-management skills in others	• **Ensures the opportunity** to do my very best every day • **Helps work group achieve its goals** by removing obstacles • **Ensures work group has tools and resources** to do job well	• **Asks about me** and how I am doing • **Ensures work group has timely, data-based performance feedback** (objective info, trended over time) • **Provides positive encouragement** for improved performance and doing the right things • **Provides constructive, pinpointed feedback** when performance is below expectations • **Directly observes work group's performance**—knows what we do

Figure 14. Sample of Q4 leadership practices

Understanding the Behavior → Results connection, behavioral leaders establish ways of measuring progress, both in behavior change and results impact.

The linkage of behavior and results makes measurement of behavior (how often a behavior occurs) a *leading indicator* of results. Broadly speaking, if the right behavior increases, results will too—so by monitoring behavior, you can predict results.

A global provider of private-label customer care learned that indicators of frontline manager behavior (frequency and quality of weekly performance coaching) predicted lagging results (customer loyalty rates, profitability) *better* than a number of traditional metrics (average speed of answer, occupancy rates, system availability). If supervisor behavioral indicators maintained or improved, operational results would follow. If they declined, results nearly always plummeted.

By monitoring weekly supervisor coaching practices, leaders could address declines in the high-impact behavior as they happened. The behavioral leading indicators proved so valuable that the company decided to base bonus and promotions decisions on them. Since managers controlled behavioral indicators better than they did certain operational metrics (e.g., system availability), evaluating performance seemed more equitable, even as it focused more directly on the primary performance drivers.

Measuring leading indicators of change enables organizations to spot shifts sooner and take timely action. In effect, behavioral indicators help to overcome the proverbial problem of "steering by looking though the rearview mirror" that accompanies an overreliance on lagging metrics (results). See Figure 15.

A caveat: Behavioral leaders don't measure behavior in all circumstances regardless of value, cost, or practicality. They measure behavior when doing so is feasible and clearly advantageous. We advise looking for the right leading indicators and including behavioral metrics when they make sense. This is likely to include situations where performers are learning new skills, when performers need encouragement to keep the

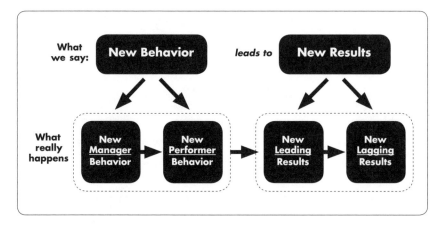

Figure 15. The Behavior → Results connection

right behaviors going, and when it's critically important to the change for *specific* behaviors to drive desired results.

STEP 7: SUSTAIN IT, IMPROVE IT, APPLY IT TO NEW PRIORITIES

What does success look like? Behavioral leaders don't define success by the initial occurrence of new behavior, or even by achievement of new results targets. They think of it as *sustained behavior change and business impact.* From the outset, behavioral leaders aim to make new habits "business as usual." They improve over time upon the initial gains, and they extend the new behaviors in new ways.

To ensure that gains endure, behavioral leaders ask themselves the following questions—and tirelessly work until they can unequivocally answer *yes* to all:

- If coaching to increase high-impact behavior ends, will behavioral and business results endure (e.g., beyond the annual plan cycle)?

- Do these gains extend beyond the tenure of one leader?

- Do results transcend the initial results targets that the company achieved?

- Has high-impact behavior generalized beyond the original circumstances or practices in meaningful ways?

- Has the organization targeted new types of business results, again based upon top strategic priorities for new competitive advantage?

- Has the organization developed entirely new types of behavioral applications over time (e.g., shaping new behavior across departmental or even customer/supplier boundaries)?

Leaders often mention sustainability, yet they behave in conventional ways that have proven again and again not to yield sustainable results.

In using the list presented in this chapter, reflect on whether your own organization asks these kinds of questions, and whether your organization is succeeding according to these criteria. If not, chapter 10 describes practices that behavioral leaders use to effect enduring and expanding change.

• • •

Most leaders lack the vocabulary and proven methods to understand and change behavior they grapple with every day. Capturing the profoundly practical logic of behavioral leadership, the seven essential steps offered in this chapter comprise pathways for turning common sense into what companies need it to be: common practice. Mastery of the seven steps can transform how companies execute their annual priorities (chapter 5), coach elite performance throughout an organization (chapter 6), lead large-scale change (chapter 7), transform culture for competitive advantage (chapter 8), and "break the code" for developing leaders (chapter 9). Curious? Read on!

A BIG BUY FOR POCKET CHANGE

As the leadership team applied DCOM to strengthen its business unit, key leader Sean drove action plans forward in exemplary fashion—until the team committed to increase use of positive encouragement to employees for doing the right things. Clearly uncomfortable, Sean acknowledged being raised under a command-and-control leadership style by his military father. He saw "positive encouragement" as unnecessary coddling and a sign of weakness. Asked how often he recognized someone for a job well done, Sean replied, "I guess never."

Sean agreed to try giving more frequent encouragement, and he devised an ingenious trick. He began each day with four quarters in his right pocket, and his goal was to go home with them in his left pocket. To move a quarter from one pocket to the other, he had to give someone positive feedback for something meaningful—four times a day, every day.

Within days, Sean found it easier to encourage people. Within weeks, his efforts were making a difference. He spent less time following up on deliverables and resolving operational issues. His direct reports were anticipating needs and generating ideas for improving the organization.

One direct report received a complimentary voice mail from Sean, which the employee then played for his family. Another said she had planned to leave, but decided to stay because Sean was now appreciating the difference she made. Within months, Sean no longer needed the quarters. He actually enjoyed providing daily encouragement. Quite a buy for a little pocket change—that he didn't even spend!

➲ THE BEHAVIORAL LEADER'S SNAPSHOT SUMMARY

In brief:

The behavioral leader's Seven Essential Steps are:

1. Target the Business Opportunity and Desired Results
2. Pinpoint the High-Impact Behavior
3. Understand the Drivers
4. Implement the Behavior Change Plan
5. Continuously Improve Your Own Leadership Practices

6. Measure Behavior Change Progress and Impact

7. Sustain It, Improve It, Apply It to New Priorities

Ask yourself:

How well do you and your leadership team . . .

☐ Establish specific goals that are clearly linked to the high-impact behavior required to meet them?

☐ Skillfully pinpoint the critical few high-impact behaviors at a given point in time?

☐ Deliberately analyze the antecedents and consequences of undesired or suboptimal behavior?

☐ Deliberately plan effective antecedents and consequences to motivate desired behavior change?

☐ Regularly discuss your progress toward motivating discretionary performance, as opposed to mere compliance?

☐ Regularly discuss improvement in your own leadership practices?

☐ Measure behavior change as a leading indicator of subsequent results impact?

☐ Plan for, budget for, and measure sustainability?

☐ Extend behavior change skillfulness and execution excellence in every successive deployment cycle?

CHAPTER FIVE

⮑ GAME-CHANGING PLAN DEPLOYMENT

Steve Jacobs, Annemarie Michaud, and Karen Bush

What is a power, but the ability or faculty of doing a thing?
What is the ability to do a thing, but the power of employing the
means necessary to its execution?
— ALEXANDER HAMILTON

Each year, companies develop a business plan that establishes priorities and deployment approaches. Leaders conduct this exercise to focus the organization and align people and resources so the company can execute well. *Yet annual plans usually fail to deliver.* In many companies, an initial focus on a critical few priorities becomes blurred, with other distracting priorities cropping up. Execution frequently suffers, and the company falls short of its plan and its potential.

The first underlying cause for failing to achieve plan comes from the numerous, often conflicting demands on middle managers. These managers are pivotal for connecting the activities of the workforce to the strategies and plans of the organization. Yet competing demands—like corporate initiatives, local strategic plans, annual production targets, competency-improvement plans for their own functions, solid-line plus dotted-line reporting requirements, and their own annual professional goals—pull them into a whirl of mixed messages they must navigate.

The second underlying cause for missed delivery of plans again comes from that neglected game-changer—behavioral leadership. Few leaders identify or use the critical behaviors that keep the workforce focused in the right direction and create the behavior changes needed to execute. Leaders who have a natural bent for behavioral leadership do get better results. But what happens when they leave? Execution and results suffer. So behavioral leadership also can be the key to building the organization's execution capability in a way that transcends changes in leadership.

Imagine focusing your entire organization on the few items that matter most, and then getting legions of managers and employees to do the right things—behaviors—in concert. Some organizations are indeed mobilizing in this way through behavioral leadership—year after year, every team, every person. They are integrating Applied Behavioral Science into their annual business cycle, making behavioral leadership the way they do business.

If you're considering where to build and leverage behavioral leadership capability, your annual plan deployment process is a great place to start. Even incremental improvement in focusing the organization and getting employees and managers to exhibit the right new behaviors leads to materially different outcomes. The behavior breakthrough in business planning and execution changes the game.

This chapter explores how a leading-edge business unit of a Fortune 50 company *behavioralized* its annual plan—with startling operational and business results. We'll then describe the executional process that underpins behavior-based plan deployment in this and other leading companies—a process for behavioral execution that we call the *MAKE-IT*® process. Finally, we will offer six tips that behavioral leaders can use to continuously sharpen their organization's execution capability year after year.

THE EXECUTION CHALLENGE

As we saw in chapter 1, most senior leaders lack faith in their organization's ability to execute with the requisite pace, consistency, and impact. While leaders cite many reasons for poor execution, we find that the following shortcomings prevail.

At the planning table:

- Senior leaders fail to illuminate the critical few move-the-needle priorities that the company *must* achieve yet will find *difficult* to achieve in the coming year.

- Senior leaders neglect to identify which of these critical priorities are the organization's BRAVO goals, that is, the top priorities that will require significant behavior change. (We use the term "BRAVO goals" throughout this book to distinguish the highest priorities of an organization that require significant behavior change to achieve success. BRAVO is an acronym for Behaviorally Reinforced Acceleration for Vital Outcomes.)

Beyond the planning table, field deployment suffers from the outset:

- Goal misalignment from the top of the organization to the bottom, and side-to-side across work units, becomes the rule rather than the exception. Goals become increasingly disconnected as they cascade down from senior leaders.

- Annual goal discussions occur within silos, further undermining collaboration. Leaders fail to specify high-impact behaviors, often overlooking altogether the need to do so. Behavior changes slowly, inconsistently, and incompletely, which means results fall short or don't last.

- Throughout the process, leaders fail to monitor how quickly and consistently people are taking the needed actions. They typically use lagging results indicators to gauge performance after it has occurred, but they rarely employ practices to ensure that execution behavior is occurring quickly and consistently.

• During execution, leaders fail to use data on progress to identify and remove barriers or to provide individual and team feedback on performance.

THE BEHAVIORAL EXECUTION ADVANTAGE: A CASE EXAMPLE

Leaders of Zenessent Industries (a pseudonym) set out to tightly link execution to their annual plan. They had three specific goals: to execute on the current year plan, manage day-to-day activities, and achieve a small set of complex execution objectives aimed at progressing toward long-term goals. They also wanted their new processes and practices to provide sufficient strategic focus, alignment, and accountability without new burdens on the workforce.

The program they implemented, *Behavioral Execution,* unfolded progressively. Execution became the collective purview of the business unit's senior leadership team. Each year, they developed the annual business plan from the strategy and then had functional leaders develop and prioritize the execution objectives. The team selected some needle-moving execution objectives, identifying where the entire organization could focus to maximize performance, both short- and long-term. They also highlighted from one to three BRAVO objectives that required significant behavior change across large groups of people. One member of the senior leadership team assumed the accountability for managing and reporting back to the team on cross-functional efforts to achieve BRAVO objectives.

Leaders then achieved alignment through a congress of the unit's senior leaders, middle managers, and relevant subject-matter experts—around a hundred people from various units. They identified specific behaviors needed to seize business opportunities, particularly the BRAVO goals. They also developed high-level team performance plans and optimized resources to achieve results. Then they finalized an execution plan to ensure both vertical and horizontal alignment.

After the meeting, Zenessent's leaders used the skills, tools, and processes of behavior-based execution (chapters 1 through 4 and augmented here and in later chapters) to engage the organization, track progress, maintain focus on goals, optimize resources, and identify and remove barriers throughout the year. Behavioral trend data and project team updates fueled discussions at leadership meetings, allowing leaders to accelerate behavioral change, recalibrate priorities, and optimize resource allocation.

Managers went far beyond setting priorities. They helped teams define workflows needed to achieve those goals as well as identify the behaviors needed from leaders and key performers to realize business outcomes. They defined leading (predictive) and lagging indicators and held reviews of progress on those metrics to recognize progress and troubleshoot barriers. By taking a behavioral approach, leaders could integrate workflows, technology, and behavior to get the right things done correctly. A clear vision and strategy would translate into specific, accountable objectives for each workforce member.

Behavioral Execution in Zenessent's Logistics

Over a period of years, Behavioral Execution became instrumental at Zenessent, yielding significant returns in cost reduction, profitability, and safety. Leaders targeted and achieved the most critical priorities within one or two years, especially those requiring large-scale behavior change. Efforts toward identifying BRAVO goals proved essential, but field deployment thereafter proved even more important. This success spurred the other business units in their division to adopt Behavioral Execution. Collectively, the divisional senior leaders have standardized on Behavioral Execution as their way of doing business.

Let's take a closer look at how Behavioral Execution has succeeded in one vital area of this organization's business—logistics.

At the peak of the recent recession, Zenessent's leadership identified a BRAVO goal for their annual plan: lowering cost and improving safety of logistics. Historically, the division rented vehicles and their operators, with vehicles sitting idle over half of the time, and vehicles in service less than half loaded. The overall logistics bill, in the hundreds of millions, crept upward yearly. Further, when vehicles were involved in an accident, the company could do little about it since they neither owned nor staffed them.

Leadership felt that centralized management of logistics would improve scheduling and front-end workflows, with cost savings and better safety performance. But they didn't know how to make this happen. That's where Behavioral Execution came in, helping them implement a new and better workflow, complete with underlying behavior changes.

A year later, leaders had begun to crack the code. Better vehicle utilization and management meant that the company had to charter a dozen fewer vehicles a month, resulting in steeply reduced man-hours. Fewer vehicles combined with the creation of a core fleet of vehicles and crew cut safety incidents in half, with no lost workdays. The unit used its vehicles nearly three-fourths of the time (up from about half of the time before), contributing to a one-third cost reduction—a *quarter-billion dollars in annual savings.*

Veteran executives couldn't believe how fast and well they had implemented the strategic plan. The operations manager remarked, "I was amazed that the team was able to change how vehicle logistics has been done for three decades. In less than one year, the change has delivered tremendous financial and significant safety improvement results."

Behind the Results

The logistics workflow involved multiple work groups, outside vendors, and even other Zenessent functions, all of which had to change how they worked. The design team created cross-functional workflows that identified each time a step required someone to perform a significant new behavior. For instance, service requesters—anyone who needed warehouse materials moved—needed to submit a request and queue up pickup or delivery within a certain time window. Warehouse personnel needed to mobilize vehicles as scheduled and monitor vehicle movement via a website.

Other stakeholders helped identify new behaviors needed for the new workflow's success. All behaviors mattered, but some high-impact behaviors mattered more than others. For instance, it was absolutely vital that service requesters sent formal requests, because the workflow depended on those requests for consistent performance. If service requesters missed the request window or made informal requests outside of the process, scheduling would not work efficiently.

Behavior Change Plans

Next, the team posed a key question about each high-impact behavior. "If we ask people to perform this new behavior—but do nothing else—is it likely to happen?" If not, designers had to find ways to change behavior.

The behavior of "service requesters submitting requests before the deadline" demanded significant change in how people did their jobs. Company culture tended to accept last-minute requests—just the opposite of the planning behavior necessary for the new workflow. Employees would need to learn a new system and embrace a new level of planning. Since people performing this behavior would see little or no immediate payoff for themselves, just asking them to change wouldn't work. The team needed a behavior change plan to make the change possible.

So, leaders created behavior change plans for all high-impact behaviors that were unlikely to happen on their own. These plans identified what would enable the performer to perform a particular behavior—like clear expectations, new skills, and new tools. The behavior change plans also identified how the organization needed to encourage a new behavior—for example, by giving positive feedback when someone performed it. Leaders were ready to make the high-impact behaviors of the new workflow come to life.

Tracking the Metrics of Progress

To monitor how well the company was reducing cost and improving safety, managers tracked leading metrics like the number of requests made within the deadline and the percentage of requests that met this target. They also tracked lagging metrics, such as the productive utilization of vehicles, and they shared all this data weekly with the entire organization.

Supervisors used this data to lead discussions during weekly meetings. When employees made a request within the deadline, supervisors called it a "green"; requests that came in after the schedule had been created were designated "red." During the meetings, supervisors praised service requesters who made "green" requests but they took care not to punish "red" requests (they didn't want people to regard the data as a punitive tool). Instead, they led team discussions about what, if anything, employees could have done to avoid the "red" and what they could do to avoid future "reds."

Coaching Supervisors' New Behaviors

Not having led discussions on behavior and planning requests before, supervisors needed to understand the data, present it so people saw the story rather than numbers, and use the data to engage their teams in productive discussions. Behavioral coaches helped by meeting with the supervisors weekly and preparing them to use the data in team meetings. They also observed meetings and gave supervisors feedback on how well they had used metrics to engage their teams. Selecting the right internal coaches also lent credibility to the entire new workflow.

Leadership Involvement

After a year, Zenessent's Behavioral Execution was succeeding, and leaders knew one key reason why: leadership involvement. The top leader set the direction publicly, and the project's executive sponsor—a member of the senior leadership team—became a hands-on participant. As the transportation manager observed, "Our sponsor's consistent involvement helped us build collaboration by engaging leaders to address potential barriers quickly."

Leadership's support proved especially important a few months into deployment when metrics still showed inconsistent results. Some service requesters were submitting requests on time, but others were leveraging long-term relationships with warehouse buddies to circumvent the system and sneak items late onto vehicles. This allowed them to avoid a "red" request on the team's metrics without changing their own planning behavior. Yet unless their behavior did change, the new workflow never would take hold and the unit would never realize efficiencies.

At a meeting, leaders wondered openly about the project's chances of success. "Our guys are just so used to submitting requests on the spot as business dictates," one said. "They're not used to planning. I don't see this changing—at least not as much as we think it will." The team recognized that business considerations would prevent employees from planning 20 percent of the work, so they set a new goal of planning only 80 percent of the work (down from the original 100 percent). With this more realistic target, even the most skeptical leaders could more actively support compliance and collaboration. Shortly after this meeting, the preplanning of work and the submission of requests by employees rose sharply.

Getting to the Right Consequences

The ability to arrive at the right consequences also proved key to Behavioral Execution's success. If a job ran ahead of schedule, enabling the unit to release expensive equipment early, then making a "red" request to retrieve that equipment was the better business decision. Yet employees sometimes didn't make such requests for fear that this would hurt their team's metrics.

To correct the perception that management always desired 100 percent green, the leadership team began to acknowledge people who made "good reds"—a schedule-interruption request driven by a good business decision. Supervisors also adjusted the conversations they had with teams, taking care not to punish people who were doing the right thing for the business. Being able to learn from and respond to these bumps drove the right behaviors and results.

Consistent Communication

A third key factor in the project's success was consistent communication. The project sponsor, project manager, and other key leaders met weekly, affording themselves ample opportunity to make decisions, break down barriers, and adjust course. Internal coaches attended weekly team meetings, learning firsthand about barriers and successes experienced by service requesters. They also met regularly with the leadership team, learning about project decisions, technology, and other support.

Coaches used their unique access to project leaders and end users to accelerate communication between centralized project management and geographically dispersed service requesters. If service requesters had trouble with a computer system, coaches took it to the IT representative on the project team. This constituted a quick, natural communication link, making it easier to remove obstacles to the new workflow.

Finally, project leaders' consistent attendance at weekly meetings proved helpful. As one noted, these meetings were "a time to understand and address obstacles—to make the key decisions necessary to keep the project moving. If we missed a week, we'd end up with a backlog that would obstruct progress and potentially discourage people who were working hard to make this change happen."

GETTING IT DONE: THE MAKE-IT PROCESS FOR BEHAVIORAL EXECUTION

Behavioral leadership confers an advantage in part by providing a logical, practical, proven methodology for superior execution of the annual plan.

Distilling thousands of hours of research and experience, we have created and deployed the MAKE-IT process for organizational execution. This process is adaptable to any organizational change or execution situation. It conceptualizes strategic initiatives as rolling out in four distinct phases or milestones: MAKE-IT Clear, MAKE-IT Real, MAKE-IT Happen, and MAKE-IT Last (Figure 16).

Making It CLEAR

In this first phase, senior leaders set the stage for successful execution by communicating the change clearly to everyone. Leaders link the change to new competitive advantage and results targets, frame the desired patterns of future behavior, assess drivers of current and desired behavior, and establish a deployment road map that addresses each DCOM cornerstone—Direction, Competence, Opportunity, Motivation (chapter 3). Leaders enlist the extended leadership team (typically their direct reports and other key stakeholders across the organization), and take time to ensure understanding, alignment, and commitment to proceed. Finally, senior leaders begin modeling practices they expect from other leaders and managers and sharpen their own effectiveness as executive sponsors, setting the stage for subsequent phases.

Making It REAL

The drilling-down that occurs in this second phase makes the change real to everyone. Leaders ensure that managers and supervisors are ready to lead broad-based behavior change. Leaders deploy a map of high-impact behaviors for all roles and levels, training managers and assigning specific behavior change plans for each manager to implement. Managers develop these behavior change plans themselves for their areas, reflecting the behaviors they will shape and building in deliberate antecedents and consequences to foster discretionary performance over time.

Leaders also develop leading and lagging metrics to track progress.

1 MAKE IT® **Clear**

Prioritize. Clarify desired performance for competitive advantage.

- High-Impact goals prioritized in annual plan
  - 1–3 most critical identified
  - Degree/difficulty of behavior change identified for each
- Key gaps and drivers understood (via DCOM®/E-TIP Analysis®)
- Success measures & DCOM execution roadmap established
- Extended leadership teams aligned and skill-building underway

Senior leaders aligned on BRAVO goals & metrics?

2 MAKE IT® **Real**

Align on High-Impact Behaviors℠. Prepare leaders to execute.

- All levels of organization aligned on key performers' High-Impact Behaviors℠ and targeted results
- Leading and lagging metrics developed, and readiness of progress-tracking tools verified
- Organizational processes aligned (minimum critical)
- Managers prepared to implement behavior change plans

Managers ready to execute with "new behaviors"?

3 MAKE IT® **Happen**

Execute. Use data-based feedback to get results.

- Managers consistently effective in shaping discretionary performance of desired behavior patterns
- Obstacles routinely removed; enablers routinely provided
- Behavior and results data routinely reviewed by managers, leaders
- Senior leaders model and reinforce desired behavior, as well as stay the course

Behavioral leadership successfully used to achieve targeted results?

4 MAKE IT® **Last**

Embed and Sustain behavioral leadership into routine business processes.

- Sustainability plan and accountabilities in place
- Organizational processes further aligned to make it Last
- Behavioral indicators routinely monitored
- Next-level behavioral leadership capability developed and leveraged for enterprise advantage

Highly engaged performance is business as usual?

Figure 16. The MAKE-IT process for behavioral execution. (The "MAKE-ITS" are a trademarked service of CLG, with milestones based on CLG's Performance Catalyst® methodology for achieving sustainable organization-wide behavior change.)

They change organizational processes and policies to eliminate obvious misalignments with the desired performance and culture and provide necessary organizational enablers.

Making It HAPPEN

Now it's execution time as managers deploy their behavior change plans. To help themselves along, managers seek feedback and coaching to sharpen their skillfulness and address obstacles to behavior change. They discuss progress metrics and key learnings in team meetings at all levels and reward forward momentum. Senior leaders continue to model desired behavior and celebrate progress, signaling their clear intent to stay the course.

Making It LAST

Finally, sustain the change—make it stick. This phase focuses not only on sustaining the desired behavioral changes but also on broadening and deepening the advantage that has been realized. Leaders establish sustainability plans and accountabilities, monitor cultural and behavioral indicators for slippage, and augment organizational processes even further to support continuous improvement. Most important, they establish new targets for achieving subsequent BRAVO goals and for further evolving behavioral execution where appropriate.

SIX TIPS TO BETTER PLAN DEPLOYMENT

Companies that have behavioralized their approach to plan deployment have greatly improved their business results and softer measures like employee satisfaction and retention. Here are six tips for executing better than the competition.

Tip 1: Start Early and Use an Annual Planning Calendar

Knowing that the right planning, with the right involvement and communication, can boost subsequent deployment, behavioral leaders schedule annual planning events to allow sufficient time for considering behavior change implications at every step. They also use a well-documented, annual planning cycle to do so. A governance structure that promotes accountability by senior leaders through routine reporting of cross-functional alignment, milestones, and progress is essential.

Tip 2: Start at the Top

Ensure complete alignment among the executive team members, and then among the next two levels of leaders, on the annual priorities overall and especially the BRAVO goals. Beyond setting aside time, this requires open and candid discussion regarding trade-offs and implications across varied (and sometimes competing) interests.

Tip 3: Use High-Impact Behavior at the Planning Table Too

Leadership team decision making at the planning table itself constitutes a type of performance-related behavior, and some companies have carefully identified high-impact behaviors for such settings. These behaviors could merit their own chapter, but a few noteworthy ones include communicating openly and helping others do the same, discouraging and redirecting deflection behaviors (e.g., responding in generalities to a specific question), distinguishing facts from mere perceptions in one's arguments, and discussing how goals relate to results metrics.

Tip 4: Set Reasonable Stretch Goals

Behavioral leaders set goals that reflect the organization's capability at a given annual deployment cycle. When facing triage conditions, they establish stretch goals that focus on establishing safe and reliable operations. If the organization is underperforming but under control, then more aggressive performance goals become appropriate. Only when the organization is performing reliably does the senior team aim to seize new competitive ground.

Once leaders establish annual goals, they watch and listen to confirm that they have set goals appropriately. Judging their 100 percent target as unreasonable and unwise, leaders in the earlier logistics example revised the target. Employee engagement and operational performance improved soon after—because employees had regarded the 100 percent target as unreasonable too.

Tip 5: Ensure True Cross-Boundary Collaboration

As important as it is to achieve complete vertical alignment on key priorities and high-impact behaviors, horizontal alignment across group boundaries remains at least as important (and perhaps tougher). Knowing this, Cadillac Fairview executives decided to strengthen their behavioral execution capability one step at a time. During their first planning cycle, they focused on enhancing vertical alignment and challenging themselves at the executive level to improve their own horizontal alignment.

During year two, the executives engaged greater horizontal alignment within the next two levels of leadership. They shifted their annual planning milestones to ensure that the executive team developed enterprise objectives ninety days prior to the new fiscal year. Sixty days prior to the new fiscal year, officers convened to focus on developing horizontal alignment of top priorities across their groups. The executive team identified points of strategic interdependence between groups and asked their officer group to identify how horizontal-collaboration agreements would confer new competitive advantage. In effect, the group clarified points of collaboration for their needle-moving priorities. The high-impact collaborative behaviors they then embraced proved especially powerful.

Tip 6: Build Behavioral Execution Capability in Successive Cycles over Time

Behavioral leaders seek improvement in steps or stages over a three- to four-year period, building a level of simple, practical behavioral adherence so that the types of practices described previously become business as usual. Companies can make important strides in their first annual cycle, but usually more opportunity for building and leveraging remains. Zenessent, the company we discussed in this chapter, concluded that increasing execution capacity would require four distinct phases over a period of years (Figure 17).

In Stage 1, Emerging: Building the Basics, leaders establish the vision for competing on behavioral execution, engaging the organization's top hundred leaders in this vision, and implementing basic processes and meeting structures.

Stage 2, Progressing: Developing Application Expertise, focuses on developing new skills and common processes across the organization's top hundred leaders while leaders execute move-the-needle priorities.

In Stage 3, Sustaining: Leveraging the Behavioral Leadership Advantage, behaviorally based processes and practices that had already added value thoroughly cascade down to the front line.

In time, the organization hoped to enter the fourth and final stage, fundamentally transforming the business for a new competitive advantage. During this stage, the focus shifts to enterprise execution. Among other things, the company strategically nurtures new behavioral leaders for the future.

• • •

As we've seen in this chapter, behavioral leaders intentionally build distinct planning and execution capability as a source of competitive advantage. Though skillful behavioral execution may not be flashy, it certainly sets companies apart. How many companies can truly say that they gain full, shoulder-to-shoulder alignment on a small set of top priorities among

Stages of Behavioral Execution Maturity

Stage 4—Extending: Building Enterprise Advantage
- Target new areas, new applications for growing enterprise capability
- Redeploy proven behavioral leaders and align stretch assignments
- Deploy proven practices across enterprise

Stage 3—Sustaining: Leveraging the Behavioral Leadership Advantage
- Routine targeting of increasingly game-changing BRAVO goals
- Routinely effective cross-boundary collaboration
- Accelerated behavioral leadership becoming business as usual

Stage 2—Progressing: Developing Application Expertise
- Annually prioritize BRAVO goals (the critical few requiring significant behavior change)
- Develop leaders as behavioral leadership sponsors and coaches
- Routine meeting structures and leader practices for reviewing & accelerating progress

Stage 1—Emerging: Building the Basics
- Align extended leadership team around direction for behavioral execution advantage
- Establish multi-year road map and align annual planning calendar
- Establish governance, process, roles, and tools

Stage 0—Strategic Weakness
- Insufficient prioritization of "critical few" goals or required behavior change
- Insufficient goal alignment (vertical or horizontal)
- Slow, inconsistent, or unsustained execution

Figure 17. Stages of behavioral execution maturity

senior leaders and then throughout the organization? How many ensure that every person—including senior leadership and managers—knows their one to three high-impact behaviors to achieve their most critical goals? How many routinely achieve what they set out to accomplish? How many get better and faster at doing so every year? As one operations director remarked, "In the past, we basically rolled the dice in comparison to the way we operate our business today." Behavioral leadership had become their routine way of doing business.

Improving annual plan deployment is only the beginning. Regular coaching is central to encouraging consistent execution behaviors. Some companies have taken yet another step and have asked themselves, "What would happen if we regularly coached for elite performance, and what if we did this at every level of the organization?" As we will see in chapter 6, the answer they arrived at is compelling.

⊃ THE BEHAVIORAL LEADER'S SNAPSHOT SUMMARY

How Does Your Execution Approach Compare?

To assess the effectiveness of your execution cornerstones, consider the following:

- **Ensuring clear, aligned Direction**
    - Does your organization translate its vision into overarching objectives and a long-range plan?
    - Does the annual business plan clearly communicate the vision?
    - Does the plan reflect business opportunities that strategically move the organization along its migration path?
    - Have you identified one to three move-the-needle priorities to direct focused action in the current year?
    - Does an individual member of the senior leadership team have accountability for each of those move-the-needle priorities— for managing cross-functional alignment and reporting on progress, especially leading indicators?
    - Have you identified high-impact behaviors (including leader

behaviors) for each move-the-needle priority in which behavior change is critical?

○ Have you articulated clear expectations for all leaders in prompting, reinforcing, and sustaining meaningful behavior change, as well as removing barriers?

○ Have you framed clear expectations for all leaders both to achieve strategic objectives and deliver on the current year plan?

○ Are you measuring and monitoring progress for all teams and leadership groups involved in moving the needle?

- **Developing needed Competence**

○ Are all leaders fluent in vertical/horizontal goal alignment and metrics-discussion skills?

○ Are all leaders and employees fluent in cross-boundary collaboration skills?

○ Are senior leaders skillful and consistent in demonstrating behaviorally based sponsorship practices?

○ Are all leaders fluent in Q4 Leadership and "coaching for elite performance" skill sets?

- **Providing the right Opportunity**

○ Have you established behaviorally based planning processes, roles, milestones, and meeting structures?

○ Have you established monthly leading/lagging progress-review reports, including behavioral trend charts when appropriate?

○ Have you designed standing leadership meetings to enable the right amount of airtime and appropriate discussion of move-the-needle priorities and high-impact behavior changes?

○ Have you discussed and resolved barriers to performance?

- **Motivating discretionary performance**
  - Do you base discussions on both leading and lagging indicators, or do you fall back on opinions and impressions?
  - Do you hold regular discussions in senior leadership meetings that reinforce high-impact behavior changes and move-the-needle achievement?
  - Do you see visible evidence of progress on top priorities, including behavioral trends?
  - Do you review and discuss the impact of leader behaviors on move-the-needle progress?
  - Do you reinforce leaders who push top priorities while also delivering on other business and maintaining appropriate workloads within their area?
  - Do your formal performance management, recognition, and reward systems reinforce achievement of high-impact behavior change and move-the-needle priorities?

CHAPTER SIX

⮑ COACHING FOR ELITE PERFORMANCE

Steve Jacobs, Paula Butte, and Mona Malone

Have you ever seen a winning team that has no coach? You cannot perform with excellence unless you have a coach. Even people who are the best, the top 1 percent or 2 percent in their field, still have a coach. Ironically, in business, we are expected sometimes to play without a coach. That's not the best way to play, either in sports or business. Business is a team event. Winning is about execution, so performance coaching always has a role. I can see people performing better because of the coaching.

— SENIOR EXECUTIVE, GLOBAL MANUFACTURER

Bedridden and in his final days at age 101, Roman Totenberg, the renowned concert violinist and teacher, received a visitor. Mr. Totenberg had agreed to give a final lesson to Letitia Hom, an accomplished violinist in her own right. Though Hom had performed Brahms's Violin Concerto hundreds of times, she sought Totenberg's help in improving her performance. Totenberg conducted in silence while she played, gesturing to slow the pace at certain points. When she finished, Letitia lowered her ear to

Mr. Totenberg's lips so that she could hear his final, whispered words of advice: "The D was flat."[1]

Musicians around the world revered Mr. Totenberg as a coach of elite performance. In most fields, coaching (by whatever name) so begets excellence that performers find *not* having a coach—and a distinguished one at that—unthinkable. Elite performers in sports and arts understand that coaching confers a vital competitive advantage. It's important that businesses and business leaders partake of this advantage too.

How many managers today provide consistent, skillful performance coaching? One study found that only 26 percent of managers coach performance routinely. Some managers regard coaching as an important part of their role but feel they do not have time. Others confuse *performance coaching* (coaching to near-term business results and behaviors) with *performance management* (formal performance reviews), blurring things further by equating performance management with end-of-year reviews (which, by the way, occur only 78 percent of the time in the average company).[2]

Behavioral leaders keenly value performance coaching. They regard it as job one and work hard to master specific coaching skills grounded in behavioral science. Behavioral leaders also understand the advantage that emerges when leaders and managers throughout a business unit prioritize skillful performance coaching, and when they pursue it according to a common approach.

This chapter offers a brief overview of performance coaching, explains why most coaching initiatives come up short, and offers coaching tips for elite performance. We also tell the remarkable story of a top-ten bank that implemented coaching down its management spine, achieving extraordinary results.

WHAT EXACTLY IS PERFORMANCE COACHING?

Performance coaching is a *structured dialogue that recognizes excellence and achieves business goals by specifying areas for improvement and learning.*

Managers who coach others do so to help them develop new skills, initiate a desired competency or goal, stretch performance to the next level, or redirect behavior to solve existing problems.

Performance coaching must occur regularly and consistently, not just once or twice per year. The cadence can vary—twice weekly in a high-volume customer service operation, for example, or monthly in a project-based technology company.

Performance coaching resembles the after-action discussions that an NFL quarterback and his coach might have each Monday morning during the season to review video from Sunday's game. Typical conversations cover behaviors to continue and the "critical few" behaviors to change at any moment in time.

Although these conversations include feedback, they go beyond mere feedback talks in the following ways:

- Feedback focuses on *past* behavior, but performance coaching focuses on *future* behavior.

- Feedback talks about "what, so what, now what." Performance coaching is about solving problems and removing barriers to performance.

- Feedback is mostly about telling, but performance coaching is more about asking and discussing.

People who receive performance coaching usually look forward to it, knowing that it has the power to make them even better at what they do, thus opening up opportunities.

AIMING AT HIGH PERFORMANCE FOR BUSINESS RESULTS

Unlike other processes, *performance coaching focuses explicitly on business results.* Performance coaches spend most of their time discussing high-impact behaviors and linking them to results. They aim not just at addressing performance problems per se but more often at achieving *high* performance and reaching a person's full potential.

Many executives have trouble understanding how to coach for high performance. Giving feedback to an underperformer is straightforward, but *how do we help already strong performers reach the next level of success?*

This question came up when we convened fifteen company leaders to discuss their progress in performance coaching. The group agreed that performance coaching afforded competitive advantages, and that they should personally set the example. They had struggled, however, to make the time and feel comfortable as coaches. Curiously, they discovered that they had spent nearly all their coaching time on the bottom 10 percent of performers among their direct reports.

We asked whether they regarded this allocation as appropriate. Initially, they nodded yes. In their view, 70 percent of their managers were solid performers who "didn't need fixing." When we asked what type of attention the top 20 percent of their managers received, the bemused response was, "more work."

Pushing back on this view, we asked the executives how they supposed the coaches of professional sports teams allocated their time. Did they typically spend 100 percent of their coaching on the weakest 10 percent of their players?

Turning to their own commitments for the coming year, the group agreed to schedule monthly coaching discussions with all direct reports and reconvene in six months for a progress check. Did the group expect to adhere to this plan? we asked. The executives fell silent.

"Look, I'll be honest," one finally said. "The reason I don't coach most of my managers, and I'm sure my colleagues would agree, is that *I don't really know what to say that will be helpful.* Most are already doing well."

We asked this leader to name a strong performer that most in the room knew, and to describe what practices made this person so valuable. Since professional hockey was popular with many in the room, we asked, "Would you say that this person is already at the very top of his game? Is he the Wayne Gretzky in that role in your industry?"

The leader shook his head. "Of course not. Not yet anyway. He's only been in the role for four years."

"Suppose, then, that you were his coach, and your task was to help him become the elite performer in that role in your industry. What would you focus on, and where would you start?"

The leader then articulated specific and very practical ideas for how his manager could take his game to the next level. As all of us in the room realized, such ideas had been there all along; only the leader's own focus and perception had changed.

And that's the first step to coaching for elite performance: Don't simply aim for strong performance; take the highest possible performance as your standard and help even high achievers excel further.

THE BANK OF MONTREAL'S COACHING SOLUTION
by Mona Malone

How can an organization skillfully build coaching into its management spine? And does such capability really translate into better performance in the marketplace? Let's take an extended look at the experience of Canada's oldest and North America's tenth-largest bank, Bank of Montreal (BMO).†

In 2010, BMO provided seven million customers with retail banking, wealth management, and investment banking services at a thousand branches across a geographic area larger than the United States. BMO's

---

† Established in 1817, BMO Financial Group is a highly diversified North American financial services provider. With more than 47,000 employees, BMO provides millions of customers with a broad range of retail banking, wealth management, and investment banking products and services, through the following operating groups: Personal and Commercial Banking Canada, Personal and Commercial Banking U.S., Private Client Group, and BMO Capital Markets.

BMO Personal and Commercial Banking Canada serves more than seven million customers, offering a full range of financial services that include solutions for everyday banking, financing, investing, credit cards, and creditor insurance, as well as a full suite of commercial products and financial advisory services. BMO Personal and Commercial Banking provides customers with an integrated network of BMO Bank of Montreal branches, telephone banking, online banking, and automated banking machines, along with the expertise of mortgage specialists and financial planners.

strategy was to compete and win by becoming the best "relationship bank" in North America—the bank that went beyond good customer service to define a great customer experience. The size of the prize? Hundreds of millions of dollars in increased revenue.

Ensuring consistent service across every customer touch point in a vast banking network demanded special leadership. BMO needed to develop more than a thousand leaders capable of ensuring consistent service and of elevating performance results at the hundreds of local branch locations. Previous training programs and sales-support models had mixed results in producing a strong performance lift across the branch network. The bank had also implemented distributed-sales-support models, set service standard guidelines, and increased the leadership capability of the management spine, but performance still varied widely across the system.

To improve customer loyalty and enhance revenue growth, BMO sought to do three things. First, it needed to align leaders around execution. One branch manager noted, "When you're trying to improve many business metrics, it's hard to know where to start. Do I focus on improving revenue, service standards, or my referrals? How do I create a sense of focus for my team?" BMO sought to cultivate more leaders who understood the highest-impact behaviors that would affect business growth and customer loyalty—leaders, in other words, with the ability to translate a business metric, like increased wealth balances, into specific behaviors. In addition, leaders who already did achieve strong results needed to learn techniques for replicating the results given a workforce with natural turnover.

Second, BMO needed to enhance how well local branch leaders changed behaviors in their teams. As another branch manager shared, "Every meeting and conversation, I tell my team that our focus is the customer loyalty measure in our branch. I don't understand why we are not seeing more traction." A sales rep in that branch made the "why" clear: "We have scores that measure customer loyalty. But I'm not sure how I really impact them." The branch manager was reinforcing the message, but the customer service representative did not understand what to do differently to influence the results. BMO needed to develop line leaders with a stronger understanding of the behavior-results connection.

Finally, to increase ownership and engagement among employees, BMO needed to make managers more coachlike. Managers had to learn to model more emotional intelligence, including genuine listening, curiosity, and accountability. Research has shown that during stressful times, leaders often don't listen to line employees when they describe the obstacles impeding their work. Feeling unheard, employees develop "learned helplessness," throwing up their hands and saying, "I work hard, but I don't know how to get the outcomes my boss wants—it is not possible." As one area manager said, "This was about me changing how I led—getting out of my office and onto the floor to observe, guide, and coach my teams. I saw many issues that I could only understand from actually being out with my sales force."

Coaching for Performance

To gain traction on these objectives, BMO adopted a three-part internal coaching program called Coaching for Performance. The program included the following:

- **Alignment mapping**. BMO already had a well-defined strategic-planning process aligned with the vision of "great customer experience," yet senior leadership was not sufficiently aligned on focus. The mapping process would reveal gaps and ensure full buy-in. The entire management spine would be called upon to help select and validate behaviors for the map.

- **Building coaching capability**. BMO would provide classroom training for all levels of the management spine, followed by eight touch-point conversations and feedback between each manager and a skilled internal coaching adviser. The bank would use specific criteria to select and train highly proficient coaching advisers.

- **Measuring and sustaining**. BMO would measure progress by tracking the managers' fluency, frequency of behaviors, and early business-results indicators. To help sustain the change, BMO would embed coaching advisers within the business.

The Toronto Pilot

BMO rolled out Coaching for Performance in 2010, testing it in a business unit with strong growth and leadership, the 2,000-employee Toronto division. Since leaders of this division were already engaged and committed to high-quality execution, positive results from the program would boost overall business results.

BMO selected coaching advisers for their business acumen and strong coaching capabilities, and it trained these advisers in the science of behavior. Alignment mapping proved harder than expected, with managers questioning the time investment. Still, working through the top business outcomes and goals eventually brought managers into strong alignment. Toronto selected *wealth balances* (i.e., increases in investment sales and renewals) as the primary objective, one with which every leader could relate. Wealth balances fluctuate seasonally, and BMO wanted to keep the momentum of high revenue levels during the year.

The leadership team completed alignment mapping and translated business objectives into behaviors by role. They then trained branch managers, area managers, and VPs to coach these pinpointed behaviors. Since needs-based customer conversations were essential to BMO's business, the bank trained employees in the "customer conversation" process and tools. The behavior chosen for financial services managers was to identify a savings and investment need during client sales conversations and discuss the opportunity with clients.

If managers consistently identified and pursued additional sales and referral opportunities, the Toronto division would move the dial on its wealth balance business goal.

Early Challenges

Two months into the pilot, the Toronto SVP—one of the company's most disciplined sales leaders—noted the difficulty of maintaining the rigor of the coaching discipline. Would the leaders have the resolve to stay with the program?

Two elements wound up helping. First, rigorous measurement allowed leaders to set realistic expectations regarding the time required to see behavior change and corresponding business results. Second, managers turned stories from leadership into a high-impact video shared at sales meetings across Canada. Local managers found it compelling to see company leaders reflect on how coaching practices had helped them do their own jobs better. Coming away from this video, they felt more skilled and capable as they participated in their own coaching sessions.

Senior leader role-modeling proved even more important as the process unfolded. Leaders who modeled the targeted coaching and feedback behaviors spread adoption down the spine, producing superior business results and higher employee engagement. One branch manager reported that "as a result of the new coaching techniques we learned with emphasis on behavior, my branch won the District Retirement Savings campaign for best year-over-year improvement in investment sales. We focused on actions and the results that followed. I coached my managers to call customers daily, and sales representatives were coached to ask every customer if they had made their retirement savings contribution. We met at day's end to share successes with the actual behaviors."

Measuring Results

BMO extensively measured the program's results. To measure changes in leadership behaviors, the bank monitored 1:1 coaching and side-by-sides for frequency and quality of execution. The bank also observed performers' behaviors to ensure sufficient frequency and effectiveness. Finally, leaders monitored leading indicators (behaviors) and lagging indicators (results) of business performance. All along, the bank's personal and commercial banking senior executives drove measurement by communicating their need to hear about program results.

The pilot succeeded. Over the eleven weeks after classroom training was completed, the pilot group increased investment sales by 125 percent and wealth referrals by 119 percent, significantly above national averages. The team was getting traction, employees were becoming more energized, and managers were feeling more capable (Figure 18).

The chart in Figure 18 was nicknamed "the hockey stick." When the chart was shared with bank leaders across Canada, many leaders asked for the training and support for their own "hockey sticks." The pilot's success triggered a full-scale, national rollout. BMO trained a cadre of internal resources, creating a full-time senior adviser for each division to sustain the gains.

Realizing that BMO could also leverage a behavioral approach to execute core work processes better, a leadership team from across the

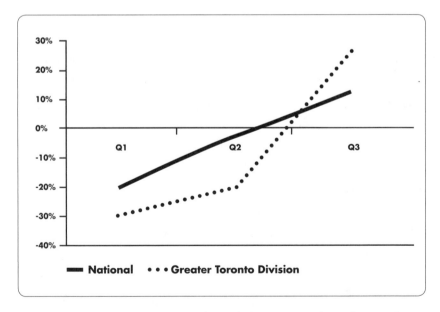

Figure 18. F2010 year-over-year change in investment sales and renewals. Pilot: 55 percent change since program launch.

enterprise met in 2011 to define and validate several high-impact behaviors linked to the managerial chain of accountability (activities like sales meetings, team huddles, walkabouts, and coaching). Today, all managers along the spine know what "good" looks like, and they are observing, coaching, and giving feedback on a standard national behavior set for all roles. In 2012, the bank began integrating the behavior/results approach into change-management and process-design work streams.

Two years after implementing Coaching for Performance, program leaders attended a sales conference in British Columbia, including branch managers, area managers for personal and commercial banking, and the senior leadership team. Six leaders who had achieved the greatest increases in customer loyalty scores—over 50 percent in a year or less—shared the best practices that led to their outstanding results. Their secret? They passionately believed in the importance of customer loyalty, and they had applied the approach of coaching for behavior change. As program managers agreed, company leaders had aligned around customer loyalty, and now they were aligning behavior at the front line around this goal too.

During the two years of the program, one company division rose from dead last in business results to second. As the recently appointed executive for this division related, "I thought I was an experienced coach and good at developing people, so when we first rolled this out, I was a bit skeptical. But I started hearing stories from area managers about their coaching impact and from frontline employees saying they now knew they could make a difference with their customers. The employees had made the behavior-results connection in terms of customer experience and growth. I attribute a lot of our improvement to Coaching for Performance."

• • •

Why Most Coaching Fails

Not all coaching is the same. Many organizations undertake some type of performance-coaching initiative, but few do it well. Despite training, managers' coaching skills generally remain low (due to a lack of practice, feedback, and reinforcement). Despite defined processes and tracking metrics to ensure reliability, managers tend to pick and choose (inconsistently) what they do to coach performance and when.

When companies allocate internal support to help managers improve coaching effectiveness, the support personnel often end up doing much of the performance coaching themselves. Even when companies expect managers at all levels to adopt coaching practices, senior managers assume that they have a "free pass" and that performance coaching is really the job of managers closer to the front line.

With companies rarely observing the quality of performance coaching and managers sometimes exaggerating their time reporting on coaching activities, leaders often don't understand the nature of coaching actually taking place. Coaching discussions tend to focus on too many things at once ("list management" rather than performance coaching), and coaching objectives often vary from discussion to discussion and between employees and managers. Often, companies fail to pinpoint new behaviors or align them with move-the-needle priorities.

Companies need to define the skill set of performance coaches, fixing on a clear method—and one that works better than the alternatives. One element of the skill set is making the Behavior → Results connection apparent throughout the coaching conversation. Coaches need to follow up training with consistent practice, useful feedback, and sufficient encouragement to continue. They need to skillfully pinpoint the right new behaviors. And they need to take a longer-term perspective on progress. Coaching takes time away from other things, it can feel uncomfortable, and it can prove hard to do well. In behavioral terms, these are Timely, Important, and Probable discouragers. Unless equally influential encouragers are introduced (e.g., short-term wins, meaningful skill-building support, and recognition of progress), managers will move on to other pursuits.

We should add that "sheep dipping" (i.e., sending scores, or hundreds, or thousands of managers through events en masse to get things started) does not build culture or competitive advantage. When managers haven't taken time to create an effective program, multiplying the number of managers involved only compounds the problem.

Even companies that have implemented coaching well on a small scale often fail to embed performance coaching throughout the enterprise. Role modeling at senior levels remains spotty, discouraging managers further down the ladder from sustaining coaching practices themselves. Meanwhile, organizational processes continue to reward the same old, unhelpful managerial behaviors. Few penalties accrue for managers who do not coach or who coach poorly, and bonuses and promotions reflect little consideration of coaching excellence.

IMPACT COACHING FOR ELITE PERFORMANCE

Here are some practices that behavioral leaders use to implement performance coaching successfully in an organization.

Behavioral leaders make sufficient time to coach elite performance routinely, changing their own practices when necessary and striving to become more skillful over time. Their clear, systematic coaching process incorporates the four cornerstones of sustained high performance (DCOM) as well as the science of behavior change (chapter 3).

One such process is the IMPACT[SM] coaching model that has contributed to a number of the company successes described in this book.[3] IMPACT is an acronym for key coaching practices that include (Figure 19):

- **Identify and Measure desired business results**. This includes linking organizational priorities to specific work group and/or individual targets and metrics, building goal alignment within and across work groups dependent on one another, and inspiring a sense of purpose and pride regarding the importance of achieving the targets.

IMPACT℠ Model

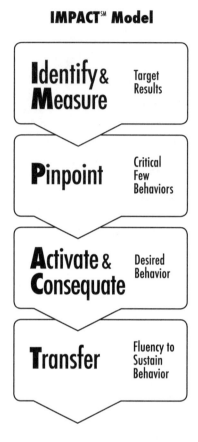

Figure 19. The IMPACT model

- **Pinpoint high-impact behaviors most essential to achieving targeted business results.** This includes analyzing the influences on current and desired behavior (the ABC/E-TIP Analysis) and developing specific coaching action plans and indicators of behavior change.

- **Activate and Consequate discretionary performance of desired behavior.** (*Consequate* means to add consequences to a behavior.) This includes implementing effective triggers for new behavior, removing barriers that impede sustained high performance, personally observing performance when feasible, participating in structured, data-based coaching discussions and following a 4:1 ratio of positive to constructive feedback, and aligning other consequences when appropriate (organizational, peer, self, natural).

- **Transfer successful approaches to achieve new progress.** This includes embedding effective consequences to become business as usual, coaching new next-level skills and behaviors, and targeting new business results (e.g., as part of a new annual plan or as a next-phase deployment of existing strategic change initiatives).

A single leader who coaches for elite performance can make a big difference within an organization. Yet the real power comes when companies share high-performance coaching capability *across all managers and leaders.* Since most companies don't do this, scaling high-performance coaching is a significant source of advantage, available for the taking.

Companies that effectively scale and leverage coaching capability typically:

- Focus coaching on new organizational performance and new strategic advantage

- Establish clear roles and accountabilities for coaching at each level of the management spine

- Map strategic imperatives to high-impact behaviors to establish the primary focus of managers' feedback and performance coaching

- Align high-impact behaviors upward from performer groups through each level of leadership (e.g., the health-care insurance company described in chapter 2)

But that's just the beginning. To scale coaching well, companies also define the performance coaching process and skill sets, describing specific, proven practices underpinned by the science of behavior change. They'll follow training or managers with action-plan implementation, regular check-ins (with observation, feedback, and reinforcement) for the subsequent four to six months, and certification of coaching effectiveness.

They'll ask senior leaders to role model effective coaching. They'll track coaching across the leadership team, looking out for weak adopters. Finally, they'll make a leader accountable for monitoring sustainability processes and metrics over the long term.

BMO's efforts have paid off in tangible business results, but their journey isn't over. Recently, a senior executive responsible for sales force effectiveness said, "I need this to be a habit, I need it to have habit strength." To that end, the company continues to focus on coaching excellence as a core leadership capability.

Here is a word of advice from a BMO leader: "Hang in there. It's like learning a new sport. I appreciated having a coach to get me there because I was uncomfortable and didn't see results right away. But, boy, when the results came, I was motivated to be the coach I can be."

• • •

⊃ *THE BEHAVIORAL LEADER'S SNAPSHOT SUMMARY*

How Does Your Approach to Performance Coaching Compare?

You won't know what you're really getting from your coaching efforts today unless you ask (and measure). Here are five things to look for:

1. **If your company has already undertaken a coaching initiative, did it start off on the right footing?** New results require the right new behavior, and highly effective starts of new behavior require three conditions working in tandem:

   - *Clear direction*—including what specific feedback and performance-coaching practices are expected, why, when, how frequently, and how effectiveness will be assessed. The most successful initiatives also ensure that each leader develops a specific coaching action plan for immediate and targeted application of the coaching skills covered in training.

- *Skill building*—which includes skills training, of course, but should also include follow-up development and certification (when desired). For instance, highly effective initiatives often require six to eight one-hour progress reviews and observations with each leader during the first four to six months following the skills training.

- *Clear opportunity*—including sufficient time to do what is expected, plus budget to support follow-up progress reviews and continued skill development.

2. **Are you getting the feedback and performance-coaching behavior you need?**

   - Is there early evidence of attempts to demonstrate expected practices? By most/all leaders?

   - Is the behavior occurring frequently and consistently enough?

   - Is the behavior occurring effectively enough? (*Tip:* Be sure to assess the extent of weak adoption and nonadoption, in addition to strong adoption. Remember the health-care insurance company described in chapter 2? Despite the overall impact on both business results and employee engagement, leaders found that even with follow-up on development and certification, 10 percent of managers remained nonadopters, and another 40 percent were weaker adopters after the first cycle.)

3. **Are the right consequences in place to encourage what's needed?** This means both formal and informal, to encourage continued growth in feedback and performance-coaching habits for each leader until it becomes business as usual for him/her. To be truly effective, the consequences for improving the rate and quality of feedback/coaching should be highly encouraging (E-TIP):

   - Positive

   - Timely

   - Important to the feedback receiver

- Highly **P**robable (likely to occur). (*Tip:* It's also important to ask similar questions regarding consequences for weak adoption and nonadoption. Are there **T**imely, **I**mportant, and highly **P**robable consequences in place to discourage weak adoption or nonadoption? Examples of consequences: asking "skip level" questions to verify if leaders are in fact providing meaningful feedback and coaching on a consistent basis; personally acknowledging leaders who are skillfully demonstrating the practices (and personally speaking with those who are not doing so); regularly discussing deployment progress, key learnings, and business/cultural impact in staff meetings and other public forums; consistently and explicitly weighting leaders' performance coaching impact in annual reviews and bonus or promotion decisions).

4. **Are you getting the business impact you seek when you need it?**

   - Measurable results (e.g., faster deal closing, more successful product introductions, improved quality performance, greater yield from Lean Sigma initiatives)?

   - Lift in employee engagement?

5. **Are organizational processes in place to sustain the gains for a period of years?** Examples might include a process to cascade skill development down to frontline management; metrics to assess ongoing adherence; a systematic approach for up-skilling leaders/ managers who are new to the business unit.

CHAPTER SEVEN

➲ CHANGING THE WAY ORGANIZATIONS CHANGE

Tracy Thurkow, Julie Smith, and Steve Jacobs

Not only must we change, we must change the way we change.

—GORDON R. SULLIVAN, FORMER US ARMY CHIEF OF STAFF, REFLECTING ON THE FALL OF THE BERLIN WALL[1]

Change in an organization is always hard, but this one was really tough and required a special touch. Following a merger, our client was shuttering a premier research laboratory after seventy years of meritorious service. For the change to proceed smoothly, our client needed to keep research proceeding efficiently within deadlines, maintain accurate records, keep key professionals on staff until the final closure date, and ensure that valuable knowledge possessed by these veterans was transferred to the acquiring organization.

One problem: Of the laboratory's more than eight hundred employees, many of whom had worked for more than twenty years with the company, 90 percent were being laid off. The loyalty people had long felt toward the company was replaced by shock and worry for the future.

The change did not begin well. It got off to a rocky start, with people calling off sick more often and missing important research milestones. Of special concern was the information-transfer process, which was not collecting truly critical knowledge because the forms given to employees asked for the wrong information.

We'll finish that story shortly, but first let us reflect on the difficulties inherent in any substantial organizational change. Senior leaders must not only foresee and plan for strategic changes but also lead execution of these changes, often before others in the organization experience much reason to do so. Most leaders would argue that *execution* is the most difficult task. How do you grow new markets, acquire and integrate a competitor, or implement new technologies quickly, consistently, effectively, and sustainably across thousands of employees? Large-scale organizational change threatens to undermine focus, performance, and morale. At least at first, employees may greet it with confusion, reluctance, or outright resistance.

Statistically, the success of major change initiatives continues to disappoint, hovering around 50 percent, depending on which study you examine (e.g., IBM, *Making Change Work 2008*; Economist Intelligence Unit, *Leaders of Change 2011*). As the CEO of a Fortune 500 recently told us, "I am amazed at the amount of time it takes to effect change. I know I might be impatient, and I can become frustrated, but I would like to see change . . . occur more quickly."[2] Or, as another senior leader put it more succinctly, "The only people that like change are wet babies." In 2010, CEOs in one survey named excellence in execution and consistent execution of strategy by top management as their top challenges.[3] More recently, CEOs reported that their biggest concerns included "redesigning the business for a different future" and "managing organizational change in a rapidly changing industry."

Organizational change at its root requires successful behavioral change. As one executive put it: "We have a history of failed cultural initiatives, which have been conceived at the top and then quickly cascaded. We must approach this change differently. *We must change how we think and how we act, starting at the top* [emphasis ours]."

This chapter applies the core knowledge and methods of behavior-based execution (chapters 3 through 6) to the special demands of large-scale organizational change. We contrast the behavioral approach to two existing approaches, the traditional project-management approach and the change-management approach. As we argue, no single approach fits all solutions. Change works best when leaders choose the right path, given the kind and extent of behavior change required. To increase the chances of success, leaders must ensure that they, members of the project team, and leaders responsible for execution understand the level of behavior change required—and just as important, their own roles in encouraging those behaviors.

PARADIGMS OF CHANGE

Consultants and other experts have traditionally advised leaders to delegate the hands-on work of change to others. But in today's fluid environment, when the challenges of aligning thousands of employees around the globe are so daunting, leaders play a more active role, particularly when the company requires significant behavior change. In the past, this might have been thought of as micromanaging. Not anymore.

Of course, not all leaders are experienced or sophisticated in managing change. Some just "do" change in the way that feels right to them, unaware of the science of behavior. The following basic strategies capture the common ways that many leaders think about and execute change:

- **Inspire people and the groundswell of change will occur.** This strategy relies on a leader's charisma to capture people's hearts and minds and in the process prompt people to act in ways that benefit the business.

- **Tell people about the strategy and why it's important, and then have confidence that they will make the right decisions.** This strategy assumes that smart people will make the right choices when faced with logical arguments about the necessity of change and begin acting in new ways that benefit the business.

- **It's my job to give them the solution; it's up to them to do something with it.** This strategy is borrowed from the Kevin Costner movie *Field of Dreams*—if you build it, they will come. Many changes that are driven out of functional groups follow this pattern. Those responsible for designing the solution, be it a new process or tool or software, do their job and then deploy the solution, assuming that leaders and employees will adopt it because it provides attractive features and benefits.

- **Senior management says we have to.** This strategy forces people into compliance with a mandate from the higher-ups. The implicit message: "We have to do this, or else there will be a price to pay."

- **Train people and they will know what to do.** This strategy assumes that given appropriate training, people will naturally begin to use new skills to perform their jobs, thereby benefiting the business.

These strategies all share something in common: They rely on people to change behavior when asked. Please change your behavior, because you love to work for me. Please change your behavior, because it's the right thing to do for the business. Please change your behavior, because you have to. Please change your behavior, and here is a tool to help you.

We can also discern two primary organizational approaches to change:

- **The traditional project-management approach** focuses on the basic task of rolling out the solution. Key activities include designing a well-developed solution, following a systematic rollout plan, providing upfront technical training, and telling people to adopt the new design.

- **The change-management approach**, usually adopted when leaders expect significant resistance, emphasizes the fostering of understanding and buy-in. Change designers develop leadership support for the change, provide ongoing communications, strategically involve stakeholders, and address emotional resistance, including use of change-management training.

In both approaches, leaders usually create the case for change, set expectations about timelines and budgets, make decisions, and monitor leading and lagging metrics. However, what a leader does beyond these basic responsibilities depends on the situation and the approach chosen to address it.

THE OLD WAY VERSUS THE NEW WAY

Both approaches can disappoint in some circumstances because, even with the best intentions and great resources, sometimes more attention needs to be paid to the balance of consequences that shape behavior. Consider two generic buckets of behavior, "the old way of doing things" and "the new way of doing things." The old way is usually pretty effective and has worked for some time. Performers have experienced plenty of encouraging consequences (**T**imely, **I**mportant, and **P**robable) from many sources (their peers, their bosses, their performance reviews, the weekly performance reports, etc.). In fact, consequences sometimes strongly discourage people from behaving in any way *other* than the old way.

Example: Project Administration Outsourcing

Administrators in one company who spend their days tracking down details and expediting actions to keep projects on schedule will receive many consequences from managers encouraging detail-oriented behaviors. Perhaps the greatest consequence of all is the pride they feel at being on top of things when answering questions about the project.

What happens when the company outsources project administration to a partner so as to increase the number of projects completed without increasing payroll? In-house project administrators are going to have to operate more strategically and trust their outsourcing partners to handle the details. An important consequence no longer exists. The old way won't quite work anymore.

In this instance, the new way requires not only a shift in behavior, but also a shift in encouraging and discouraging consequences. Antecedents that occur before behavior to prompt or kick-start it might promise that the new way is worth it. But as we discussed in chapters 3 and 4, consequences that are **T**imely, **I**mportant, and **P**robable will determine whether the new way becomes business as usual.

Project administrators in our example receive a great deal of communication and training (antecedents) in their new roles, and they understand the expectations (another antecedent) for their behavior change. Unfortunately, the new behavior of turning the details over to the outsourcing partner does not come with sufficient encouraging consequences that are positive, **T**imely, **I**mportant, and **P**robable. In fact, many stakeholders within the company still expect project administrators to be on top of things, and project administrators find it incredibly stressful and embarrassing when they are not.

Example: From Number Crunchers to Business Partners

Taking another example, consider what happens when a company transforms the finance function from number crunchers (the old way) to business partners (the new way). Under the old way, business analysts create multiple versions of spreadsheets based on requests and inputs from their customers in marketing to enable decisions about products. The new way involves standard reporting, which means that the same analysts must provide their marketing customers with a preprogrammed report and offer insights but not reworked spreadsheets. This change is often referred to as "moving from ad hoc to standard reporting" and entails being a business partner instead of a transaction processor.

The old way means customers receive highly customized reports that they like and use (Timely, Important, and Probable consequences that encourage the behavior), leaving analysts feeling like they've provided great customer service (Timely, Important, and Probable encouraging consequence). The new way requires the business analysts to allocate their time differently. They will spend more time talking to their marketing customers to understand what the customer seeks to accomplish, they will be interpreting standard reports to provide value-added insights from the data, and they will be sharing their insights with customers. However, they won't be spending as much time digging through source data and reworking customized spreadsheets.

The new way requires that marketing customers think ahead about what they want to accomplish and talk with the business analyst differently than they have in the past; they no longer will have an on-call resource that will slice and dice data. If conversations between the business analysts and marketing customers become awkward or frustrating, with the marketers not receiving information they need or the analysts receiving feedback that they didn't serve the customer well, the new behaviors are likely to be discouraged. Over time, people will ignore the standard report and revert to the old behavior of digging through source data to compile customized spreadsheets.

WHO BEARS THE RESPONSIBILITY FOR CHANGE?

In large-scale change efforts, attention to consequences often slips during a handoff in the change process—from project teams creating or modifying work processes, systems, or tools to leaders and employees deploying them. During the handoff, team members usually focus on deployment and not on behavior change, with managers assuming that people will behave differently on their own (or if given proper training). Yet relying only on antecedents like training does not guarantee behavior change.

A project team tasked with capturing and deploying best practices might struggle with what "deploy" means. Does it mean "post on a Share-Point site" or does it mean "ensure people use the best practices to improve performance?" The organization wants people to use the practices but the project team might lack strategies to influence performance.

Project teams will often say, "Our job is done. We built it, communicated it, and trained people on it. Now it's the leaders' job to execute." Leaders and employees will often say, "This solution isn't realistic and doesn't account for critical factors in my business." They feel like the project team is throwing the solution over the wall at them. As a result, change happens slowly, not at all, or with costly churn.

Executives who excel at leading change know not to measure success by how fast a solution gets developed and deployed, but rather by how quickly people begin to work differently and improve results. These executives set the expectation that *the project team and leaders bear joint responsibility for ensuring that people implement change and achieve expected results.* They don't declare success when the project is deployed, but when *performance changes.*

Shared accountability forces project teams and leaders to recognize that bedrock truth: New results require new behaviors. Like it or not, an organization can't achieve performance goals until people change what they do and say.

A BEHAVIORAL CHANGE MODEL

To move from the old way to the new way, a few leading-edge companies have developed and deployed an innovative behavioral approach to change. Unlike the two approaches described earlier, this behavioral approach focuses on achieving sustained results through committed, sustained behavior. Figure 20 compares the three approaches.

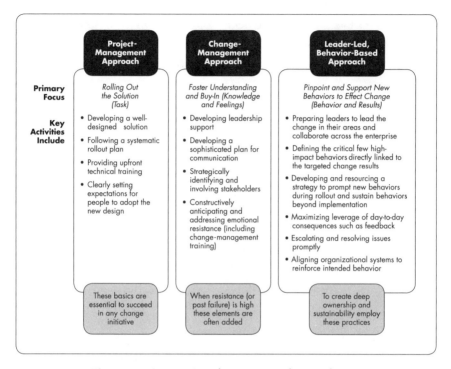

Figure 20. Comparing three approaches to change

Behavioral leaders anchor change initiatives and underlying behaviors to clear, measurable results. Using the tools examined in previous chapters, they develop a strategy for prompting initial behavior during rollout and sustaining behavior during implementation. They align other organizational systems to reinforce the intended behavior, maximize leverage of day-to-day consequences, and prepare managers appropriately.

In implementing a behavioral approach, leaders perform behavior-change planning with both the project team and leaders, asking the following questions:

- What new behaviors will the company require of leaders and employees? Which one to three behaviors are most critical? How will those behaviors generate promised results?

- Assuming perfect communications and training (and other antecedents), which behaviors will the company still have trouble generating after go-live? How will we help people perform these new behaviors? What **T**imely, **I**mportant, and **P**robable encouragers can we insert to get these behaviors going—and keep them going?

- How will we know at an early stage if these behaviors are happening?

- Have we talked with people expected to perform these new behaviors to get their take on what support they will need? What have they said?

Leaders implementing a behavioral approach hold regular team meetings. They ask how team members are working with leaders to set up a smooth implementation, and ask team members for their expectations about roles. Leaders huddle with other leaders on how they are preparing to implement the change, how they are working with the project team to ensure smooth implementation, and how they define their expectations about roles and responsibilities after go-live.

Sometimes leaders perceive such questions as micromanaging. Consultants often advise leaders not to worry about these details and to focus on setting the vision and inspiring change. Yet leading the behavior-based approach to change is not micromanaging. Helping the organization address behavior enables the organization to execute change well and reap the rewards. That is nothing other than the leader's job.

CHOOSING THE RIGHT CHANGE STRATEGY

The behavioral approach by no means comprises the *only* path to organizational change. Savvy behavioral leaders employ all three change strategies, depending on the degree of difficulty in achieving lasting behavior change. How do you choose?

Traditional Project Management

Traditional project management works best when people *want* the change and will likely adopt the new behaviors needed. In such cases,

DEALING WITH RESISTANCE

People resist change for logical reasons. We might not always see the logic because we don't have their point of view. Regard resistance as a form of feedback–often it means that the organization has not listened to and addressed people's concerns.

You can feel uncomfortable listening to people's concerns or dealing with emotions because this takes time and might create tension you are not prepared to handle. For example, if people feel upset about moving to a new location, you may have no options to offer and might not wish to spend time just letting people vent. You might prefer to keep people focused on doing their jobs, since you can't change the outcome.

But if you see resistance as a barrier, you restrict yourself, creating an unproductive "I win, You lose/You win, I lose" situation. Instead, focus on hearing concerns and helping people look at options they can control. If people feel upset because the new location is farther away and increases their commuting cost, you might encourage carpooling or other options within their control. People can find realistic solutions, even if you can't change the facts.

At the outset of change, ensure that people have a chance to ask questions and raise concerns, and managers are prepared to welcome that instead of fighting it. If you view concerns as problems to resolve together, you can create a win-win situation, even when the change is difficult.

new behaviors tend to be pretty obvious and easily learned with minimal technical training, and plenty of encouragers exist for the new behaviors.

When people receive a cell phone upgrade or sales kit update, or when they are asked to use a new file-sharing service, leaders can focus on rolling out the solution to people who are ready to receive it—or who can be made ready easily. Leaders can succeed primarily by mapping out the project plan, communicating the goals, and training people in new skills.

Under the project-management approach, leaders should ask these questions to ensure successful change:

- Are we sticking to the project plan?

- When people learn about the change, do they seem eager for it?

- When people come out of training, are we seeing the behavior change we expected? How do we know for sure?

- After people have been out of training for a while, do they have trouble keeping the behavior going?

Change Management

Companies turn to *change management* when they expect strong emotional resistance. When companies downsize, move to a distant building, or lose a valued benefits package, traditional project management can inflame the situation because people perceive that leaders don't care about them. They feel change is happening *to* them rather than *with* them. Rolling out the change makes people feel "rolled over."

Leaders should focus on addressing resistance so people will become ready and willing to accept change. This largely entails leaders listening to employees and addressing questions and concerns. Leaders also must equip people with skills to increase their personal resilience and anticipate what it will take to retain key talent during this difficult time. As one global leader remarked, "Some people when facing an organizational change at the top of the house will take the announcement very hard, and we must be sure to keep their heads and hearts engaged."

Leaders can succeed by engaging local managers in managing resistance, using frequent two-way communications when the change is announced, and providing change-management training to leaders and employees.

Leader-Led, Behavior-Based Change

The behavior-based approach works best when behavior change will occur with difficulty across a large number of people. Leaders pinpoint specific behaviors needed to maximize results and encourage those behaviors. Success depends on careful behavioral planning, preparing employees and leaders to observe and encourage behavior, and addressing systemic consequences (measurement, incentive, performance-management systems) that might impede new behavior.

Choosing a change strategy requires ascertaining how difficult the behavior change will be. If you expect a difficult process, focus on articulating the case for change, clarifying expectations, and arranging resources. If you expect great difficulty, invest time and energy in enrolling people in the change (sometimes in groups, sometimes in private 1:1 conversations), clarifying desired behavior changes, personally observing and reinforcing progress, and encouraging other leaders to do the same.

In every case, you must ensure that the organization is really ready to have desired behaviors happen on day one *and* become business as usual. If you do that, you can feel confident that the company will achieve desired business goals.

BRINGING IT TOGETHER

With large initiatives, the project team sometimes has to muster more than one change approach. For example, a company sought to save an estimated $50 million by replacing computers across 200 sites (averaging 150 units per site) and changing from on-site support to a centralized helpline. The project team knew some users really wanted the new units, which were faster. For this population, the project-management approach worked fine. Implementing the change only entailed communication and a little technical training.

For other users, the magnitude of the change seemed much greater. Some employees were using highly customized programs for which no program documentation existed. With the new computers, these users would lose their custom programs and use alternatives approved for the entire corporation. To address this complication, the company deployed the behavior-based approach.

Leaders first pinpointed specific behaviors critical to success. As the project team did not know how to influence these behaviors, they worked to identify Timely, Important, and Probable encouragers for three performer groups: site managers, cutover teams (who would physically change the units), and users.

The single most critical behavior to achieving the implementation goal was *site managers submitting specs for the needs at their sites.* Prior to the changeover, the project team conducted problem-solving sessions with site managers, emphasizing the importance of getting their site specs in on time.

The project team created two very powerful encouraging consequences for this behavior. If a site manager provided the specs on time, he could choose what to do with the old units. Some site managers were excited to donate them to a local charity, while others looked forward to auctioning them off to employees. Second, the site manager received a personal email from a member of the executive steering committee thanking him for supporting the initiative.

Cutover teams needed to perform two critical behaviors: They had to spend no more than an hour on each changeover, and they had to use customer service skills to create a positive user experience (by building trust with the user, they would make the user more likely to call the centralized helpline). To that end, the company trained cutover teams on customer service skills. At the end of the changeover, each user completed an anonymous survey. Cutover team members who achieved high levels of user satisfaction could select from a menu of awards.

For users, the business case depended on one behavior in particular: After accepting their new computers, they had to call the helpline with questions, instead of bothering the cutover team during the changeover. At the end of the changeover, a video recorded by the CEO popped up to thank users for their support and reinforce the initiative's importance. The CEO also acknowledged the inconveniences users were experiencing. He asked users to complete the satisfaction survey and reiterated the company's commitment to make the helpline very customer-oriented.

As a result of these efforts, 98 percent of site managers completed their specs on time, and customer satisfaction ran very high. The project team was surprised to discover that investment in the behavior-based approach yielded insights into how to encourage high-impact behaviors, including how to engage executives in providing the encouraging consequences and leadership the initiative needed to succeed.

EXTREME SITUATIONS

In cases such as this last one, applying a behavioral approach can help optimize an organizational change process where difficulties seem likely. In other instances, behavior change is so difficult that neither organizational nor typical leadership levers will bring about even modest success. Here the behavioral approach to large-scale change can prove especially helpful.

In the laboratory shutdown described at the beginning of this chapter, people were losing their jobs, experiencing sorrow and frustration, and, despite their pride in their work, feeling varied motivation to help the organization achieve its objectives. Fortunately, leaders applied the Pyramid of Consequences, so they could look beyond organizational and leadership levers to mobilize peer-based, self, and natural consequences.

Laboratory leaders pinpointed a few high-impact behaviors required for a smooth, efficient shutdown: They needed employees to come to work (absenteeism was high), stay until the end of the shutdown period (key people were departing for other opportunities), and accurately complete the knowledge-capture forms (employees were not responding well to these). Leaders then explored consequences that would encourage desired behavior despite the difficult circumstances.

An analysis of the consequences to the 800-plus employees reveals the true levers that were influencing behaviors (Figure 21).

Most of the consequences for employees originated at the bottom of the pyramid—where they are most powerful—and the consequences were *all discouraging*. No wonder change efforts weren't working. The most powerful levers were driving everyone in the wrong direction.

Leaders concentrated on aligning consequences and consequence providers so as to develop employees' discretionary performance, tap sources of peer and self-consequences, and remove naturally discouraging consequences. The goal: Get employees to "leave with pride" and leave with a "leadership legacy."

For each team, leaders inaugurated progress scorecards that addressed safety, ongoing deliverables, and knowledge transfer. They also held weekly reviews and celebration/problem-solving based on results. They launched a "leadership legacy" video and yearbook depicting the laboratory's proud history, kept bonuses in place, tripled bonuses if all team members remained until shutdown, and brought placement help on site. Finally, to ensure that researchers and engineers completed knowledge-capture forms, administrative assistants entered data based on input captured via video.

The results demonstrated the power of using behavioral science to pull the right levers. The laboratory retained 96 percent of its employees until closure and documented 100 percent of the desired knowledge and learnings from the lab. Operating costs decreased, despite added costs of administrative assistants. Cycle time to regular customers decreased over

23 percent, while customer satisfaction improved over 17 percent. Safety at the facility was the best in its history, allowing employees to receive "operational excellence" bonuses for the first time ever.

At the macro level, leaders succeeded in shifting the culture from *have to* do the job to *want to* do the job. They moved the source of encouraging consequences for desired behavior down the pyramid: from Organization and Boss levels to the powerful Peer and Self levels. They replaced negative talk with positive talk about "our legacy" via video and yearbook, thus allowing employee pride to take over.

Desired Behaviors	Consequence to Employees	Effect on Employees	Consequence Sources
1. Come to work	Hear negative talk	DISCOURAGING (Timely, Important, Probable)	Peers Self
	Delay getting on the job	DISCOURAGING (Timely, Important, Probable)	Self
	Interact with boss	(UNCERTAIN) (Timely, Important, Probable)	Boss
	Maybe get $$$ incentive	ENCOURAGING (but Delayed, Important, Unlikely)	Organization
2. Fill out forms	Boring	DISCOURAGING (Timely, Important, Probable)	Natural Self
	Pressure to make quota	DISCOURAGING (Timely, Important, Probable)	Natural Boss
	Low pride in work	DISCOURAGING (Timely, Important, Probable)	Self Peers
	Please the boss	(UNCERTAIN) (Timely, Unimportant, Probable)	Boss

ORG
BOSS
GROUP/PEER
SELF
NATURAL

MORE POWERFUL

Figure 21. Analysis of the consequences to the 800-plus employees reveals the true levers that were influencing behaviors. Note how the discouraging consequences come from the strongest sources.

ADDITIONAL TIPS FOR LEADING CHANGE

Large-scale change often brings unique challenges and complexities. Companies might appoint sponsors and project leaders to temporary governance roles, implicitly asking them to work across functions or business units through the power of influence, not authority. Sometimes companies establish separate project-management offices to govern the change effort, creating parallel organizations that might or might not coordinate well with one another. Companies charter one or more project teams to develop solutions, ending the charter upon deployment of the solution (not, as we've seen, when employees are changing their behavior and actually using the solution).

But that is not all. Important stakeholders may hold vested interests in the change that might not appear at the outset. Organizations often feel tremendous pressure to keep the project on time and budget, driving a focus on completing activities to get to go-live that might or might not result in real change.

With these challenges in mind, we can augment the behavioral tools presented in previous chapters with the following tips:

> **Tip 1**: Senior leadership should assume more responsibility for communicating the case for change in terms that help the entire organization understand what the change means to them, not just why the change is good for the business.
>
> **Tip 2**: Project teams, when they exist, should use behavioral tools such as the ABC and E-TIP Analysis to influence the balance of consequences in the design stage, as well as to clarify remaining gaps that the company cannot address by design and therefore must address as part of the change-deployment approach.
>
> **Tip 3**: Similarly, governance structure leaders and members (e.g., project-management office members) should learn and utilize

behavioral tools at each MAKE-IT phase. Line leaders, including senior change sponsors, should participate in pinpointing the leadership practices that will prove especially helpful at different points throughout the change process and devote personal time to prepare and do these things.

Tip 4: The organization should integrate specific behavioral methods within its existing approaches for developing stakeholder engagement, effective communications, and change-resiliency practices.

Tip 5: Deployment planning should transcend the traditional large-scale change solutions and include deliverables like new role definitions, communications tool kits, training, self-help tools, and so on. Such planning should ensure that sufficient, meaningful consequences encouraging the new behaviors exist at the outset of go-live.

Many organizations struggle with large-scale change—at a time when the competitive pressures necessitating change loom larger than ever. Change is never easy, but it is possible to do it well, even on a very large scale.

• • •

In this chapter, we looked at ways in which organizations can change. By ensuring that change support teams and leaders are working together to prepare the right encouraging consequences, companies can build in successful behavior change from the very beginning, diminishing the possibility of false starts, resistance, and finger-pointing, and allocating resources earlier to strategies that are more likely to encourage new behaviors. They can make a smoother transition from design into deployment planning into execution. Ultimately, by changing the way they lead change, companies can achieve what every organization wants: faster, more complete, and more engaged impact.

➲ *THE BEHAVIORAL LEADER'S SNAPSHOT SUMMARY*

How Do Your Leadership Team's Change Practices Compare?

Which of the following describe your leadership team's change practices?

- **Communicate about change**
  - ○ Regularly communicate the "why" behind change in an open and transparent way.
  - ○ Make clear what we stand to gain or lose based on how well we deliver.
  - ○ Ask for feedback about how well our teams understand the change and what's expected of them.

- **Address personal reactions to change**
  - ○ Take stock and be aware of our reactions to change.
  - ○ Ask for feedback about the impact we are having on others.
  - ○ Regularly adjust our behaviors to lead effectively.

- **Help team members adapt to change**
  - ○ Listen to and address our team's thoughts and concerns.
  - ○ Follow up one-on-one to help people who appear to struggle with change.

- **Achieve short-term team priorities and celebrate results**
  - ○ "Inspect what we expect," meeting at least weekly with the team to discuss performance and project status.
  - ○ Regularly give positive feedback to encourage the right behaviors.
  - ○ Regularly address lagging performance with individuals and insist on improvement to the expected level.

- **Retain key staff**
  - Ensure that we are aware of potential flight risks and regularly keep in touch with them.
  - Understand what motivates and engages key staff and act to ensure key staff experience those things.

- **Track and resolve issues**
  - View issues as opportunities and ask that issues be surfaced quickly.
  - Respond to "bad news" calmly and effectively, and reinforce people for not shading the truth.
  - Insist on using data and keeping the focus on what's right, not who's right.
  - Insist on quick resolution of issues and communication to all who need to know.

- **Ensure success past go-live**
  - Be clear on the few high-impact behaviors needed by key performers to create results.
  - Ensure **T**imely, **I**mportant, and **P**robable encouragers are in place for high-impact behaviors.

CHAPTER EIGHT

⊃ WINNING ON CULTURE

Steve Jacobs, Laura Methot, and Les Dakens

The thing I have learned at IBM is that culture is everything.
—LOUIS V. GERSTNER JR., FORMER CEO, IBM

Most of us know the phrase, "Culture eats strategy for breakfast."[1] But have we really internalized the idea? Business thinkers have written about culture's relationship with competitive advantage[2], but most leaders still don't commit to reshaping their cultures—and of those that do, few succeed.

Hunter Harrison is one of those few. Upon becoming CEO of Canadian National Railway Company (CN) in 2003, he faced a dilemma. Through divestitures, acquisitions, and streamlining actions, he and his predecessor had taken the company from a sluggish government-owned corporation to a more nimble public enterprise and industry leader. Yet competition was growing ever tougher. The company had no magic, no unique technology with which to outflank competitors. How would CN remain on top?

Harrison was the last person who would pay attention to something as "fluffy" as culture, yet he concluded that he would need to create advantage by transforming CN's culture into one in which every employee demonstrated initiative and leadership by innovating ways to improve execution.[3]

A stronger culture paid dividends for CN. By 2006, the company had tripled its stock value, increased its operating ratio advantage over competitors by an additional ten points, and delivered nearly twice the industry average for return on revenue. In 2007, former Morgan Stanley Dean Witter rail analyst James Valentine noted: "CN is to freight railroading what Michael Jordan is to basketball and Tiger Woods is to golf." As of this writing, CN, now led by president and CEO Claude Mongeau, continues to dominate its competitors in performance.

Harrison and his team succeeded where many others failed by applying a behavioral approach to the challenge of cultural change. We've seen that behavioral leadership enhances change processes in general, but the benefits it holds for cultural change are especially breathtaking. For a growing number of companies, the behavior breakthrough makes culture change concrete, practical, and finally attainable. This chapter describes specific behavioral methods underpinning successful culture change as well as best practices that leading companies such as CN have developed along the way.

WHAT *IS* CULTURE, ANYWAY?

We can trace the struggle organizations have with reshaping culture to one simple fact: Leaders remain confused about how to define culture. Indeed, few terms in business are as vague or slippery. One famous historical definition regards culture as "the complex whole which includes knowledge, belief, art, morals, law, custom, and any other capabilities and habits acquired by man as a member of society."[4] Sounds pretty all encompassing. What does this even mean?

Unfortunately, many organizations today use a similar definition or, less helpfully, don't define culture at all.[5] Leaders have a hard time feeling passionate or determined about changing a "complex whole" of more or less intangible things. And because leaders view culture as amorphous, their approaches to culture change become scattered and unfocused, and culture sometimes gets a bad rap as "fuzzy" or "soft stuff."

Many leaders get so frustrated that they wind up underestimating culture's relevance to competitive advantage. The corporate landscape is littered with well-intended culture change efforts that withered over time because, whether anyone said so or not, they were viewed as "nice to have's" rather than strategic imperatives.

As Tony McGuire, CEO of Irish technology firm System Dynamics, has observed, "I was initially resistant to considering the role of culture as critical to our business success. I viewed culture as 'hugging a tree' or 'going to the opera.' I had no idea how culture related to the performance of the organization."

How many of you think the same thing?

THE BEHAVIORAL DEFINITION OF CULTURE

Leading culture change is not easy, but companies that have adopted a behavioral approach to culture change are setting a standard for what can be achieved and how quickly. Behavioral leaders begin by rejecting vague definitions of culture and refusing to undertake initiatives that are merely symbolic or that amount to boiling the ocean. They define culture in a way that enables them to change it in tangible, focused, performance-enhancing, and enduring ways. Specifically, they define *culture* as:

> **A pattern of behavior . . .**
> > **that is encouraged or discouraged . . .**
> > > **by people and by systems . . .**
> > > > **over time.**

Let's consider each component of this definition. By thinking of culture as an observable *pattern of behavior* (not including unobservable thoughts, attitudes, morals, etc.), leaders can identify undesirable or counterproductive behaviors within the current culture as well as new behaviors that reflect their desired culture. They can even put their finger on the new behavior that, if demonstrated consistently, would improve competitive advantage, and they can identify when this impact would be greatest, and why.

Behavioral leaders often clarify culture change objectives by framing them as From → To themes (e.g., From a Culture of Blame to a Culture of Accountability, From a Culture of Silos to a Culture of Collaboration, etc.). They then translate the desired culture into specific high-impact behaviors throughout the organization at every level and role. Doing so enables individuals to see the important role they play in creating the desired culture, and by extension, in helping the company to succeed.

Continuing with our definition, culture for behavioral leaders is behavior that is explicitly *encouraged or discouraged.* Here behavioral leaders' knowledge of the science of behavior and ABC/E-TIP tools (chapters 3 and 4) changes the game. Rather than simply behavioralizing culture change objectives, behavioral leaders determine what factors encourage the undesirable behavior in the current culture. They assess the extent to which meaningful antecedents and consequences encourage culturally desirable behaviors and they use this analysis to establish their road map for progress.

From the next line of our definition, both *people and systems* can encourage or discourage the behaviors that make up a culture. Behavioral leaders transform culture by aligning the right balance of consequences and making smart decisions about which levers to use in doing so. To transform their culture and achieve unprecedented industry performance, Canadian National Railway leaders knew they had to change certain aspects of their formal processes and systems. But they started with a leadership strategy (new leadership practices that consistently produced discretionary performance) as the point of the spear, augmenting this emphasis over time with process and system changes as needed.

And finally, the last phrase in the behavioral definition of culture—*over time*—looms large. Common sense suggests that entrenched behavior, and therefore culture, doesn't change overnight. Thus, assessing the role that consequences play in influencing behavior enables behavioral leaders to understand the *history* of consequences in their organization. Leaders can establish a realistic timeline for behavior change, verifying if change is proceeding in the face of apparent (and inevitable) setbacks. The past doesn't have to predict the future, but it casts a shadow until more recent experiences rebalance historical ones.

MAKING IT SO

The behavioral definition of culture, along with the use of the seven key steps discussed in chapter 4, will take organizations a long way toward redressing cultural ills. But how can large organizations scale this approach across hundreds, thousands, even tens of thousands of managers and employees?

The answer: Use the MAKE-IT model for behavioral execution described in relation to annual business plan deployment (chapter 5) and in relation to large-scale change (chapter 7). The method of execution remains largely the same, with just a couple of adaptations to render the model suitable for building a winning culture.

Recall the four stages of the MAKE-IT model: MAKE-IT Clear, Real, Happen, and Last. First, in the MAKE-IT Clear stage, the senior leadership team establishes culture change as one of its top three business imperatives. They also establish From → To guideposts that characterize the current and desired cultures. In this stage, the senior team articulates *why* the desired culture will enable new advantage in the marketplace.

For a number of MAKE-IT milestones, focusing on behavioral changes that drive the desired culture can supplement other kinds of metrics. For instance, using behavioral leadership to achieve breakthroughs in time-to-market for new products will naturally pull along new behaviors in cross-boundary working effectiveness.

A BEHAVIORAL LEADER SPEAKS

TONY MCGUIRE, CEO, SYSTEM DYNAMICS (IRELAND)*

After resisting for years, I came to a conclusion: To become Ireland's number-one IT solutions company, we had to change our culture. Specifically, we needed to transform ourselves from a project-focused organization to a client-centric one.

We assessed ourselves against the DCOM cornerstones of high-performance organizations—which took a bit of courage, as we were already successful and proud of our accomplishments. But applying the "new eyes" of behavioral leadership revealed gaps. For instance, employee alignment on our company's direction was shockingly low. And despite our self-image of technical prowess, we discovered our professional competence was lagging (our people told us this themselves). And so on.

So, we launched our new client-centric culture through a unifying metric that focused everyone on delivering value to customers. We identified high-impact behaviors we needed, and then we trained, coached, and measured the occurrence of the new behaviors. This also meant realigning management and leadership behaviors through setting new objectives and performance measures, giving/receiving feedback, and delivering on all commitments.

Many doubted that we could transform the company so fast, because it involved changing behavior, processes, and infrastructure. And I personally had to show great resolve, communicate the case for change, give constant feedback, and celebrate even the tiniest progress.

* Following their culture change transformation, in 2009 System Dynamics was named a Deloitte Best Managed Company for the first time. They maintained this standing in 2010 and 2011, and in 2012 achieved the Deloitte Best Managed Company Gold Standard Award.

The turning point began when some team members saw early success and our change effort developed momentum. And we succeeded: Our mind-set moved from conservative to proactive, and what we've accomplished in the midst of a global recession would have been unthinkable with our prior culture. And I now understand how behavioral tools, techniques, and coaching are making me the most effective leader possible. I feel I've actually learned what leadership is.

Our breakthrough began the moment I realized: Culture is behavior. Behavior is culture. And that we could use this understanding to our competitive advantage. This is so important in an otherwise undifferentiated world.

That said, deciding to achieve a new competitive advantage by building an industry-leading *culture of collaboration* would likely drive a focus on additional high-impact collaborative behaviors. Behavioral indicators of progress in the MAKE-IT Happen stage and of sustainability in the MAKE-IT Last stage similarly expand to include both those related to the desired culture and those that drive new performance in general.

In adapting the MAKE-IT model for cultural change, organizations can deploy a number of tools and frameworks described in this book, including the IMPACT coaching model explored in chapter 6. Coaching supports the shaping of specific behaviors across business units, helps employees understand behavioral science tools, and enables leaders to leverage scorecards.

In organizations we've worked with, leaders have used coaching to help them develop and execute daily, weekly, and monthly meetings geared toward review of key metrics, celebration of progress, and problem solving to close gaps. Coaching has also helped leaders increase their visibility to model desired behaviors and learn how to coach for correction.

Ultimately, coaching helps leaders become fluent in a methodology for managing their business, so that they can sustain cultural transformation as new issues and challenges arise.

Because behavior change throughout an organization takes time, leaders should gauge overall progress by the stages of cultural maturity shown in Figure 22. This helps leaders understand the progress of cultural change.

As part of their annual planning process, some senior teams will target a culture change progression of one or two stages in the cultural maturity model for the next twelve months. Similarly, companies sometimes find it helpful to track each dimension of their cultural change objectives (safety, customer focus, cross-boundary collaboration, etc.) across the five stages of the model. Whatever the case, cultural change becomes much more tangible, manageable, and comprehensible when envisioned as a clear, close-ended process.

TRANSFORMING CULTURE AT BITUMINE CORPORATION

Let's now turn to an industry that seems far removed from the touchy-feely stereotype of culture, but where culture change is making all the difference: mining.

Alberta's oil sands contain the world's largest reservoir of a very thick petroleum-sand mixture called bitumen. Bitumen is recovered through special wells that soften the bitumen with steam, or by surface mining (as is done with coal). The material is then heated to extract the oil.

Mining Alberta's bitumen has been underway for more than forty years, but recent trends have made it even more attractive. Despite increased demand for the region's supply, one company, BituMine Corporation (a fictitious name), found itself losing ground. During its first few decades, BituMine delivered steady improvements in production volume, cost per barrel, and safety. But in the past decade, despite significant growth and investment in technology, both production and safety became less predictable, and costs skyrocketed. Injury rates increased, gaps between actual and

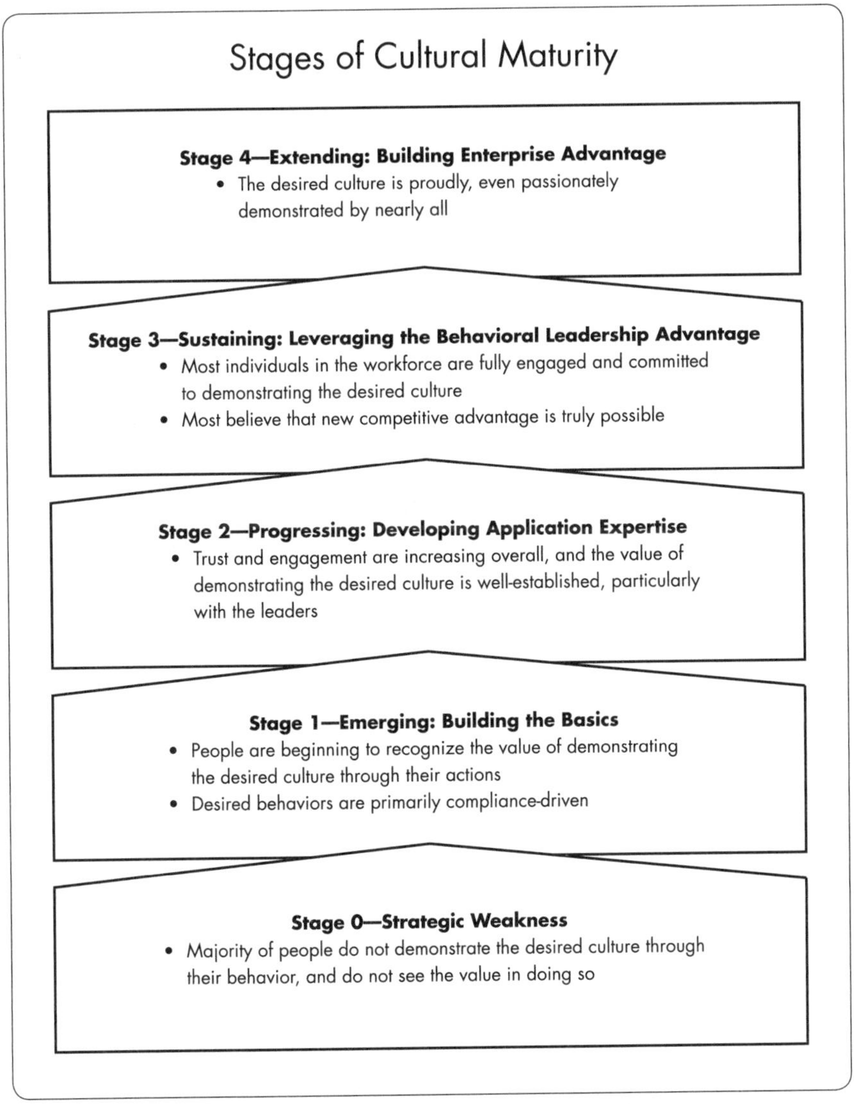

Stages of Cultural Maturity

Stage 4—Extending: Building Enterprise Advantage
- The desired culture is proudly, even passionately demonstrated by nearly all

Stage 3—Sustaining: Leveraging the Behavioral Leadership Advantage
- Most individuals in the workforce are fully engaged and committed to demonstrating the desired culture
- Most believe that new competitive advantage is truly possible

Stage 2—Progressing: Developing Application Expertise
- Trust and engagement are increasing overall, and the value of demonstrating the desired culture is well-established, particularly with the leaders

Stage 1—Emerging: Building the Basics
- People are beginning to recognize the value of demonstrating the desired culture through their actions
- Desired behaviors are primarily compliance-driven

Stage 0—Strategic Weakness
- Majority of people do not demonstrate the desired culture through their behavior, and do not see the value in doing so

Figure 22. Stages of cultural maturity model. We've deployed it in leading-edge organizations where it helps leaders understand the progress of cultural change.

targeted production widened, and the cost of each barrel produced rose by 58 percent over the previous best-cost performance. Though changes in structure and procedures to reverse performance declines had some effect, the improvements proved neither sufficient nor sustainable.

Why was BituMine really losing ground? The answer was culture. Although BituMine had fostered a culture of working hard, employees still did not deliver consistently on commitments. They also didn't understand the crucial connection between their own performance and organizational results.

As BituMine's leadership team realized, the company had developed a long-standing pattern of accepting and unintentionally encouraging missed performance goals so long as everyone seemed hard at work. Annual goals no longer held meaning for employees; it was not uncommon to hear managers communicate annual goals to their team by saying, "I know that the goals are unattainable, so just do the best you can."

The leadership team concluded that it needed to move the organization from a culture of working hard to a *culture of ownership and commitment*, using CLG's behaviorally based approach.

In the MAKE-IT Clear stage, the leadership team defined this new desired culture. BituMine's leaders then set about communicating the desired culture to the rest of the company. Using our behavioral definition of culture, they further concluded that they needed to achieve a new pattern of behavior at all levels, starting with leadership practices that would promote high engagement toward meeting performance commitments.

During the second stage, MAKE-IT Real, each operational and functional unit used behavior mapping to connect the long-term goal of safely and cost-effectively producing crude oil to the key performers who had the most impact on those goals. Finally, each unit pinpointed the high-impact behaviors that would make the results happen. The behavior map in Figure 23 demonstrates the Behavior → Results connections in relation to specific performance goals, while Figure 24 suggests the breadth of results the company sought.

Over two years, more than 3,000 frontline employees and 400 leaders from several departments worked to MAKE-IT Happen by adopting behavior consistent with a *culture of commitment and accountability.* Part of the shift entailed pinpointing the critical few new behaviors that

Targeted Result	Lagging Indicators	Front-Line Operator Behavior	Supervisor Behavior	Manager Behavior
Haul-truck Use of Availability	• Truck wait time • Operator Controlled Delays	Trucks, shovels, and dozers; monitor load, pit, road, and dump conditions, and: • Give feedback to one another • Notify supervisor of production barriers • Call dispatch if truck wait time is too long	• Review shift logs and daily plan and communicate plan to operators • Get performance data every 4 hours and give feedback/ coaching to operators • Monitor mine, identify production limiters, and intervene at appropriate level	**Production Supervisor** 1. Set direction for work execution 2. Review plan changes managed by shift superintendent and give feedback 3. Give feedback and coaching to front-line leaders about decisions made on recent shifts **Shift Superintendent** 1. Monitor work to ensure plan is fulfilled 2. Spot limiters on shift and work with front-line leaders to remove 3. Manage changes to plan based on changing conditions

Figure 23. Behavior map for haul-truck utilization, showing the connection between targeted results, lagging indicators, and the leading indicators of various employees' behavior

committed and accountable employees would do well and regularly, and quantifying the gains that would accrue from the new behaviors. Leaders then identified their own behaviors to support the frontline employees, and area teams tracked performance against targets, discussing where gaps were occurring and collaborating on solutions to reach or exceed goals.

In framing the cultural change plan, leaders applied the science by introducing practices that would discourage the prior, unwanted behavior

Key Result Areas	Targeted Behaviors (Examples)
Safety	Near-miss reporting Peer-to-peer interventions Compliance monitoring tours
Reliability	Number of saves Work order history completed Structured rounds compliance
Productivity	Job packs reviewed Pre-job site visits Cross-boundary feedback
Cost	Unit visits Plan execution

Figure 24. BituMine's targeted results

and encourage the desired culture. Over a two-year period, the company provided up to six months of IMPACT coaching to 400 leaders from sixteen departments in Production, Maintenance, and Technical, indirectly impacting 3,000 frontline employees and another 3,000 contractors. All departments followed a systematic and replicable accountability process that focused on each department's most important business opportunities. Most managers took seriously their role in shaping the culture through their daily interactions.

In order to MAKE-IT Last, BituMine adjusted processes that blocked or impeded consistent demonstration of the desired behavior pattern at each level. For instance, the organization had been working on improving its meeting structure and data usage to enhance cross-discipline alignment. Within business units, members of the production, maintenance, and engineering disciplines met to discuss area performance. By providing these cross-discipline teams with behavioral tools and approaches to enhance how members interacted in these venues, the company expanded cross-boundary collaboration and improved business-unit results.

Figure 25 offers an example of one such tool, a stewardship model for conducting cross-boundary conversations in a structured way. In further support of MAKE-IT Last, the company incorporated behavior mapping into the annual business-planning process and made the stewardship model a standard part of the way the company does business.

Linking culture change with things like haul-truck utilization (Figure 23) may seem dull, but that's the magic in the making. Rather than toy with committees and cliché solutions, BituMine's leaders aimed their efforts toward changing what mattered—the pattern of behaviors that performed and managed the organization's core work.

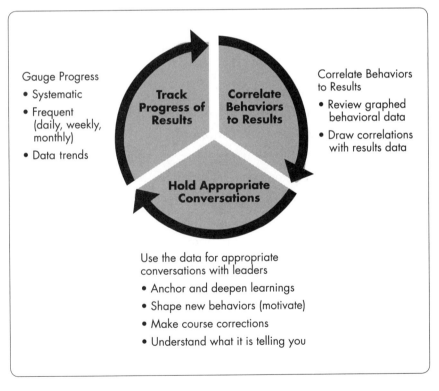

Figure 25. Stewardships provide a structured process

Less than two years after implementing the accountability process, the company saw dramatic results. Production had its best first quarter on record, and the cost per barrel dropped just over 6 percent from the same period a year earlier. Safety performance (measured by the industry standard Total Recordable Injury Rate, or TRIR) showed a more than 200-percent improvement. Aggregate cost savings across all departments after two years of implementing the culture change process conservatively yielded an estimated $400 million, with about a 30:1 ROI.

Leaders at all levels and across all participating business units and functional departments happily greeted dramatic changes in the culture, including improvements in their own leadership capacity. They improved their fluency in behavioral science and their modeling of accountability behaviors. Employees noticed and appreciated the difference. Feedback ratings verified that employees perceived managers as acting in ways that reflected a culture of commitment and accountability.

In addition to the main outcomes described here, the company realized several secondary benefits, including increased communication within teams and across departmental boundaries; improved business acumen and a better understanding of the company's business strategy; clearer relationships between frontline performance and leading and lagging business outcomes; consistent use by managers of a common leadership process and shared set of tools; and most notably, improved organizational discipline, accountability, and results focus.

Of course, managers' practices didn't become consistent or skillful on day one. Employees' behavior didn't automatically change either, nor did they come to believe that leaders were serious merely because their manager communicated something new or provided different feedback for the first time in years. *New behavior patterns took root over time as leaders repeatedly and consistently encouraged people for doing things differently.*

Leaders at BituMine created a winning culture by ensuring that the organization saw enough early progress to support continued deployment.

Compared to other alternatives, the behaviorally informed cultural change process led to rapid success. As one VP observed, "We could not have achieved in five years, with many false starts, what [the behavioral leadership approach] helped us accomplish in eighteen months."

TIPS FOR BEHAVIORAL LEADERS

Even when leaders have the right behavioral tools at their disposal, cultural change does not come easy. The following tips can help smooth the way and ensure the success of your organization's cultural change initiative.

Tip 1: Make the Commitment

Senior leaders, *you* are the architects of your company's culture. You may have inherited unfavorable conditions from your predecessors, or acquisitions may have complicated the task of shaping the desired culture, but you bear responsibility both for envisioning a new culture and for implementing processes and practices to MAKE-IT Happen. You cannot, and should not, delegate this responsibility. You need to commit fully, explicitly, and personally to building new competitive advantage through culture change.

It's not enough to treat culture as one of many levers that contribute to a company's success. You have to put culture change front and center—or risk failure. Hunter Harrison and his senior team at Canadian National Railway operated from a clear premise: "Our business success depends on motivated people who can deliver a safe, reliable, customer-focused service, while conscientiously controlling costs." CN then adopted Five Guiding Principles—Service, Cost Control, Asset Utilization, Safety, and People—and used them to drive all aspects of their culture change.

Tip 2: Don't Start All at Once

Rather than blanketing the organization with sudden waves of activity, begin with a few well-chosen pilots to fine-tune culture change methods and demonstrate meaningful business impact. Three to five proof-of-concept projects will usually work. When one of these fails, as sometimes happens, the organization can gain insights to guide subsequent deployment planning. Done well, pilots create positive buzz in the organization, lay the foundation for a deployment strategy of "pull" (as opposed to "push"), and fund the next rollout cycle through their initial performance gains.

Tip 3: Balance Enterprise Standards with Local Flexibility

In deploying across your organization, offer clear guidelines for when you expect simple replication and when you will allow innovation on the local level. Recognizing the need for both consistency and flexibility across location, CN adopted a *100 percent structure, 100 percent flexibility* deployment strategy. Certain required elements would remain constant across locations, including a focus on the Five Guiding Principles, using behavioral science to pinpoint high-impact behaviors and develop behavior change plans, and providing training and coaching to managers until they could demonstrate clear behavioral leadership proficiency. On the other hand, local groups had the freedom to prioritize results targets in their own way, to determine the process and timing for rollout, and to assign local support resources.

Tip 4: Start at the Top and Work Down

In a cultural change initiative, it's important for each level of leadership, starting at the top, to ensure sufficient clarity and skillfulness before asking the next-level managers to do their part. In DCOM terms, companies must get both Direction and Competence right before engaging the next level. For the extended leadership team, this means ensuring that each member can communicate the desired culture and link it to new advantage, personally model desired behavior patterns, and reinforce and coach desired behaviors in direct reports and others. Leaders will need additional skills soon thereafter (e.g., removing systemic barriers and aligning formal consequences to achieve E-TIP criteria), but the skills mentioned here are the most essential at the outset.

Remember, you are leading sustainable culture change for new advantage, not fixing a performance crisis. The latter requires that you target behavior change immediately at the point where performance happens. The former requires that leaders demonstrate the desired culture and skillfully shift the balance of consequences throughout the organization so as to influence the organization's performers over time. Unless senior leaders develop the right skills and behavior for themselves and their direct reports, behavior change though the organization proceeds tentatively and sometimes cynically.

Figure 26 illustrates a deployment model known to behavioral leaders as the *DCOM cascade*. The sequence of steps combines strengths of both vertical and horizontal deployment, focusing on achievement of *culture change outcomes*. These steps unfold in a distinct, logical (but to some leaders, counterintuitive) sequence that influences what performers know, feel, and do without skipping the leader preparation so essential for sustained success.

	Direction	Competence	Opportunity	Motivation
Executive Level	1 ⟶	2	4	7
Mid Management	3 ↖	5	8	10
Front Line	6	9	11	12

Figure 26. The DCOM cascade deployment strategy

Tip 5: Practice 17x17 Consistency

Not only must a manager's practices align with those of line workers across time; practices must remain consistent *across managers*. Listen to one group of managers at CN as they recall their aha moment on this point: "We slumped in a meeting room late one night amid empty pizza boxes and soda cans, tired to the bone. We had been at this since 7:30 that morning and had been on this grueling schedule for weeks. We were desperately trying to change the out-of-control elements of our railroad— people leaving work hours early, theft, low productivity.

"That night, it finally dawned on us: *We, the leaders, were the problem.* Too many of us were inconsistent in our expectations of employees. Some of us let people leave early, overlooked theft, or didn't ask people to do their best. We thought we were being good guys. If we didn't stop overlooking these actions, then and there, CN was headed for a dead end. There would be no need to continue, as there would be no way we could change the culture.

"So we took a simple oath: No one dodges responsibility. We accept our role as leaders, and this is what we signed on for. And we will hold each other accountable for doing the right thing. There were seventeen of us at the table. Someone said, *We all must agree—all seventeen of seventeen must align.* That phrase stuck. From that point on, whenever the going got tough, we'd look at one another and say, '*seventeen out of seventeen.*' "[6]

Tip 6: Use Metrics that Motivate

CN implemented Employee Performance Scorecards[7] to align individuals' performance metrics with the company's Culture of Precision Railroading objectives. Moreover, the company designed the scorecards so that managers could use them in a variety of reinforcing ways (e.g., assigning an Outstanding Railroader designation for consistently high scorecard ratings). In addition to providing the basis for regular coaching discussions, scorecards became a source of pride for a number of employees. Some employees took the scorecards home to share with their families, posting them on the kitchen refrigerator next to their children's report cards! (Railroaders have their own culture of pride that spans generations.) The scorecards have also contributed to MAKE-IT Last: At the time of this writing, six years after initiation, use of these metrics is still going strong.

Tip 7: Signal with Informal Processes Too

Conventional approaches to culture change use symbols (titles, trophies, mascots, logos, etc.) to reflect what's important to an organization. We encourage this as well. Be creative and have fun. Just remember to purposefully use symbols to prompt and encourage desired behavior.

Even antecedents can serve as especially powerful and relevant cues. As part of their commitment to modeling candor and cross-boundary collaboration, officers at Cadillac Fairview inaugurated what they called Elephant Lunches to encourage timely, candid discussion of difficult issues. In a simple, somewhat humorous way, they built upon the symbolic value of breaking bread together to initiate tough discussions. One officer jokes, "Even if the wheels come off in the discussion, you can't yell too loudly in the middle of a restaurant."

Tip 8: Get the Right People on the Bus[8]

Senior leaders who have guided culture change often wish they had addressed more quickly those individuals who had worked to derail progress. If someone persists in impeding the desired culture, leaders must ask him or her to leave the organization, regardless of role or level. CN replaced over 25 percent of its supervisory staff (through retirements, transfers, or termination) so as to improve the company's leadership practices.

Tip 9: Stay in It for the Long Haul

Building culture for competitive advantage merits regular attention over time for at least two reasons. First, as Tushman and O'Reilly point out, most competitive environments are constantly evolving.[9] The patterns of behavior that make your culture an asset today can impede long-term success if not managed well and shaped over time.

Second, a high-performance culture by definition strives for continuous improvement. Consider what Nitin Nohria and his colleagues observed in their groundbreaking research:

> Our study made it clear that building the right culture is imperative, but promoting a fun environment isn't nearly as important as promoting one that champions high-level performance and ethical behavior. These organizations design and support a culture that encourages outstanding individual and team contributions, one that holds employees—not just managers—responsible for success. Winners don't limit themselves to besting their immediate competitors. Once a company has overmatched its rivals in, say, the effectiveness of logistics, it looks outside the industry. Employees may ask, for instance, "Why can't we do it better than FedEx?" If the goal is unreachable, it still represents an opportunity for high-performing employees and managers: "If we can't be the best at logistics, why not outsource it to a partner that can?"[10]

• • •

Unlike most companies, leading-edge organizations that learn to apply behavioral leadership capability are making their culture a core part of their strategy for winning. Whether they focus on a culture of innovation, engagement, customer-focus, or accountability, they intentionally build culture as a source of competitive advantage. And they do so with novel and replicable approaches that draw upon what behavioral leaders know that others do not. The results speak for themselves.

➲ *THE BEHAVIORAL LEADER'S SNAPSHOT SUMMARY*

How Does Your Approach to Culture Compare?

Should we consider reshaping our culture?

- How would employees, customers, and vendors describe your organization's current culture? Considering the information presented in this chapter, as well as external trends on the horizon, what aspects of your culture give you a distinct advantage or threaten your competitive advantage?

Give you distinct competitive advantage:	Diminish your competitive advantage (or might in foreseeable future):
+	**–**
+	**–**
+	**–**
Consider behavior patterns such as—	
• Timely, consistent execution of key initiatives • Holding one another accountable • Cross-boundary collaboration • Customer-first prioritization	• Innovation from everyday operations • Decision speed and sense of urgency • Open communication and candor • Feedback and coaching to bring about the best • Reinforcement and high engagement

- Is there a clear opportunity to gain competitive advantage by changing aspects of your culture?

- Is the potential gain significant enough to merit Top Three prioritization for the next two to three years?

- Is this important enough to you personally to merit your active, consistent involvement for the next two to three years?

Will we win with our approach?

- Which of the following practices describe your organization's approach to building culture?

    o   We clearly link our culture change initiatives to building competitive advantage and measurable business impact.

    o   If we choose to change our culture in some way, we make it a top priority.

    o   If we undertake culture change, we stay the course, make steady progress, and achieve what we set out to accomplish.

    o   We define the specific new behaviors that our desired culture requires, and we do this by level and role when appropriate.

    o   Senior leaders are actively and personally involved in modeling and reinforcing the culture we seek.

    o   We ensure that our culture change objectives are both values based *and* results based.

    o   We routinely use leading and lagging metrics to track and review progress.

    o   We routinely surface and remove obstacles that prevent us from consistently demonstrating desired behavior patterns.

    o   Ninety percent or more of our managers do a very good job in encouraging and reinforcing desired patterns of behavior throughout the organization.

    o   Ninety percent or more of our managers do a very good job in discouraging undesired patterns of behavior throughout the organization.

    o   If someone persists in doing things that harm our culture, he or she is asked to leave the organization regardless of role or level. (We deal with this fairly and respectfully, but we deal with it.)

○ We are effective in aligning our organizational processes and policies to support our desired culture. We make the right adjustments without boiling the ocean and undertaking more redesign than is really needed.

○ We have a history of sustaining the gains we make, despite changes in leadership.

○ We have a history of continuously improving our culture, as well as further extending our competitive advantage in this regard.

CHAPTER NINE

➲ DEVELOPING BEHAVIORAL LEADERS

Steve Jacobs, Leslie Braksick, and Kathy Callahan

Developing talent is business's most important task.
—PETER DRUCKER

To achieve competitive advantage through Applied Behavioral Science, companies not only need an enhanced annual plan, culture, and change processes—they also need strong behavioral leaders.

During the last decade, one of the world's premier global industrial companies was reorganizing, changing from a regional profit-and-loss structure to global business-unit accountability. A new president who had been appointed at a key business unit faced a number of challenges. Overhead ran too high, and a number of projects were floundering thanks to poor execution. Business strategy lacked focus, contributing to low morale and questions about the business's sustainability.

As part of a broader turnaround strategy, the president decided to develop leadership capacity by providing behavior-based coaching that enhanced leaders' focus, improved organizational effectiveness, and sustained diversity and constructive tension. The president himself undertook executive coaching and required his team to do the same.

Over the next five years, the business unit saw a remarkable turnaround. The leadership team improved its strategic focus and its ability to execute. Profitability grew fivefold and safety performance improved sixteenfold on roughly the same volume of work. The unit grew into a world leader in its market and became a gemstone in the larger enterprise. All of this occurred because executives chose to do what it took to become strong behavioral leaders.

We've referred to behavioral leaders in a number of contexts throughout this book, but the time has come to focus squarely on behavioral leadership itself. We define such leadership as *the ability to foster and sustain discretionary performance of high-impact behavior change.* All behavioral leaders must motivate their people and colleagues to *want to* perform at consistently high levels. Moreover, senior leaders must have the capability to scale behavioral leadership across business units and, ultimately, across the enterprise.

What distinguishes behavioral leaders is not general intelligence, sophistication, or competence, but possession of a set of skills and abilities relating to application of the behavioral approach. Companies that seek to foster these skills and abilities must go well beyond the conventional leadership training most companies favor.

In particular, they must take leaders outside of the classroom setting and develop them in the field, where they learn by doing, every day. Leaders themselves must commit to the process of personal growth and to mastering the behavioral techniques so critical for superior performance.

THE CORE CAPABILITY OF BEHAVIORAL LEADERSHIP

Previous chapters have provided a composite picture of what behavioral leaders do and think about. Let's briefly summarize.

First, behavioral leaders apply the DCOM performance model better than most. When it comes to *Direction*, behavioral leaders articulate strategic goals and expectations to direct reports, teams, and organizations.

They do this repeatedly, to the point of boredom, realizing that clear and compelling understanding of the purpose can never be left to chance.

Behavioral leaders then ensure that the organization demonstrates the *Competence* and capability to follow the strategic direction. They sample proficiency through site visits and conversations with employees at all levels. They monitor leading-indicator data to see if individuals, business units, and the organization are performing as expected—and if not, they determine whether employees possess the *Competence* to do their jobs well.

Behavioral leaders also work to sweep away bureaucratic obstacles so that individuals have the *Opportunity* to fulfill the company's stretch goals. In their diligence, behavioral leaders ensure that core processes, tools, ways of working, time, and resources enable (and never disable) high performance.

Finally, behavioral leaders provide *Motivation* to their people. They align rewards and recognitions with organizational goals. Most important, they regard themselves as coaches, providing feedback and guidance at every turn, and developing this same capability in others. Behavioral leaders also strive for a clear picture on how they themselves are performing; this in turn allows them to hold a mirror up to people and businesses and to motivate *others* to want to be better. Behavioral leaders understand that the company will stagnate in the absence of accountability and also strong feedback that encourages continuous improvement.

Moving beyond DCOM, we've also seen that behavioral leaders distinguish themselves by demonstrating the seven steps of behavioral leadership described in chapter 4 (targeting opportunities, pinpointing high-impact behaviors, understanding the drivers, etc.). Behavioral leaders also are able to apply a behavioral capability to annual business plan deployment (chapter 5), to coaching for elite performance (chapter 6), to leading large-scale organization change (chapter 7), and to transforming culture for competitive advantage (chapter 8).

All this represents a pretty tall order. So what must a company do to grow behavioral leaders, including the senior executives who make behavioral leadership standard practice for an organization?

WANTED: (BEHAVIORAL) LEADERSHIP DEVELOPMENT THAT WORKS

One thing is certain: You can't turn to business-as-usual leadership training practices. Approaches to leadership development vary, but they offer only mixed results. One study conducted by the Corporate Leadership Council examined seventeen types of leadership development programs and found that leaders rated only six of them higher than 6.0 on a 10-point scale. Leaders viewed feedback and relationship programs (e.g., coaching, mentoring, or creating a leadership development plan) as more important than experience-based programs (e.g., working in new lines of business or in foreign countries) or education-based programs.[1]

The study also reported that companies tended not to excel in providing the leadership development alternatives leaders most valued; five of the six most highly rated kinds of programs scored in the "less effectively delivered" quartile.

Others have reached even more discouraging conclusions about traditional leadership training. Robert Kramer, principal researcher at The Conference Board, argues that half a century of research has failed to yield widely embraced, reliable approaches to leadership development that produce significant business impact and return on investment: "By all rights, we should have this down by now. A lingering leadership crisis continues to haunt the corporations of today and shows no sign of abating."

Kramer goes on to say, "The study and practice of leadership and leadership development continues to be a work in progress, albeit one that shows frustratingly little progress. Leading authorities are finally coming to terms with our lack of fundamental knowledge about these closely related fields."[2]

The inconsistent impact of leadership development programs owes in part to leaders themselves. As we mentioned in chapter 1, leaders overestimate their leadership effectiveness and neglect activities that could help them identify and improve the skills that would most benefit them. Our proprietary Q4 Leadership survey database found that leaders overrate their ability to hold themselves accountable, to observe work groups and know what people do, to collaborate with others, to take responsibility when problems occur, and to remove obstacles that impede a positive work environment.[3]

Why leaders fail to discern their own weak spots is no mystery. Some leaders interpret their accession to power as proof positive of their effectiveness. A few seem impervious to the observations and feelings of others. The higher leaders rise in the organization, the less contact they have with frontline performance, customer interactions, and employee perceptions, making it easier for leaders to misunderstand the impact of their actions. Leaders also become insulated from helpful feedback about their performance because subordinates feel reluctant to share it.

DEVELOPING BEHAVIORAL LEADERS WHILE THEY ARE MAKING IMPORTANT THINGS HAPPEN

Leaders want to excel. They accept that they have room for growth, and they are in principle willing to participate in reasonable development activities. Behavioral leadership training appeals to many leaders because, unlike traditional approaches, it focuses on learning by *doing,* on developing leadership capability *while leaders continue to make important things happen* in their organizations.

In 2008, behavioral experts Leslie Braksick and Jim Hillgren queried twenty-seven sitting CEOs about the training experiences that had proven most or least helpful.[4] Several themes emerged:

1. CEOs reported that receiving a stretch assignment, with full accountability, ahead of their apparent readiness, was paramount to their growth and development.

2. Running a stand-alone P&L was also key because it gave CEOs a place to lead and learn, to be accountable, and yet enjoy some layer of protection so they could make mistakes and learn from them.

3. CEOs found that access to immediate and constructive feedback was critical in all stretch assignments and key roles. Whether coming from a mentor, a coach, or a trusted adviser, feedback helped CEOs fuel and adjust their leadership actions.

Interestingly, CEOs did not once mention leadership development programs or courses during the twenty-seven interviews. Does that mean these programs lack importance? Absolutely not. Leadership development courses help supervisors and managers develop base skills so that they can then go on to become senior leaders. What these CEOs were saying is that the *real* learning occurs on the job, in the moment. Leaders learn most while being in the game.

The German novelist Hermann Hesse once said, "The truth is lived, not taught." Executives become proficient in behavioral leadership not by undergoing classroom training, but by living the behavioral approach in the field, applying new knowledge and methods daily toward business objectives central to the organization. Further, executives develop behavioral leadership capability by realigning reinforcing consequences in their work environment to sustain improved habits.

Think of it this way: Training does not equal skill, which does not equal consistent habits, which does not equal business impact (unless they are the right habits), which does not equal sustainability. Behavioral development approaches accomplish this complete sequence of milestones, not merely the antecedent-based activities at the outset.

IMPLICATIONS FOR TRADITIONAL DEVELOPMENT TACTICS

Behavioral leadership training typically integrates three ingredients. First, programs employ *stretch assignments* that task leaders with both achieving new organizational performance and sharpening their leadership effectiveness.

Second, they provide enough *feedback* so that executives remain keenly aware of their development targets at all times.

Finally, they incorporate the clear expectation that *leaders develop others in turn.* While this last component may seem obvious, it often fails to appear in practice. Developing others sharpens self-awareness as well as a number of the skills highlighted previously, such as observing performance, giving effective 4:1 feedback routinely, seeking and using feedback routinely, designing behavioral leading indicators, and so on.

Training behavioral leaders does not require that a company jettison programs it might already have in place and start from scratch. Companies can reshape or supplement traditional approaches such as executive education, executive coaching, and leadership team development so that they have more impact. Consider the following examples.

Executive Education that Links Field to Forum

As a recent report documented, executive education programs that address capability gaps have a tangible business impact, driving change and embedding "practical improvements across organizations."[5] Some leading institutions are taking innovative approaches that combine world-class executive education with expert execution support and behavioral leadership application in the field.

Enterprise Ireland is a government agency charged with supporting the development of world-class Irish companies. The agency helps position these companies in global markets so as to increase Ireland's economic strength and wealth. In 2005, Enterprise Ireland realized it needed to augment its strategy by also raising the ambition and leadership capability of Irish CEOs. In conjunction with the Irish Software Association, Enterprise Ireland selected the Stanford Graduate School of Business to develop a new growth-oriented leadership curriculum. The resulting program, Leadership 4 Growth, had four elements:

1. **Inspiration.** World-class CEOs would present their story to participants, as well as their challenges, strategies, and successes.

2. **Education.** Stanford faculty would teach entrepreneurial leadership theory that links insights to real-world business challenges, including presenting case studies and exploring strategies to improve personal leadership skills and define and communicate a clear company strategy.

3. **Coaching**. As part of the program, participants would receive continuous support through individually assigned coaches. The coaching would improve and strengthen individual leader characteristics and attributes within the framework of company strategy.

4. **Execution**. The program would provide continued coaching support and assignments guiding leaders in the implementation of core concepts and models covered in the program.

Unveiled first with CEOs in Ireland's software and technology sector, Leadership 4 Growth was organized into four subject-matter modules conducted over approximately a year: proactive strategic leadership; developing people assets to build high-performance organizations; business execution through strategy, leadership, and a solid infrastructure; and showcasing results and lessons so as to make the case for the company.

Between modules, CEOs completed individual and senior leadership team assignments focusing on the critical challenges for their respective companies. Additionally, and critically, CEOs met with other leaders from their cohort to discuss strategic challenges and enhance the execution of their respective business challenges.

At the outset, the program paired each CEO with an executive coach from our company, the Continuous Learning Group (CLG), Stanford's coaching partner in the program. The coach helped individual executives take insights learned at Stanford and execute them in their companies. Enterprise Ireland also provided business advisers who assisted CEOs in evaluating and prioritizing strategies, implementation tactics, and capability needs; who challenged CEOs on how they were using the knowledge, frameworks, and tools introduced at Stanford; and who facilitated monthly cohort meetings that drew upon the groups' collective experience.

The inaugural program in 2006–2007 enjoyed impressive success, creating a buzz among Irish CEOs and prompting Leadership 4 Growth to expand across additional cohorts, sectors, and partners.[6] One CEO summarized the impact of Leadership 4 Growth as follows: "This has been a catalyst and conduit for change in my whole company, bringing new

WHY I SPONSORED THE "WHAT I WISH I KNEW" STUDY OF CEOS

WILLIAM R. JOHNSON, CHAIRMAN, PRESIDENT & CEO, H.J. HEINZ COMPANY

I firmly believe that effective leadership is the difference between success and failure for most organizations. Thus, one of the greatest challenges companies face is identifying and cultivating effective leaders. Doing this well can be a significant competitive advantage.

Despite everything written about the CEO's crucial leadership role, what's been missed is the shared, collective perspective drawn from active CEOs' personal experience. I sponsored this research to ensure we had captured top leaders' candid view of what they wish they'd learned prior to their CEO role. Listening to active CEOs, we found recurring "what I wish I knew" themes, plus clear requirements for certain personal attributes, career experiences, and management practices.

Two important implications of this work need emphasis. First, more leaders need to realize that doing the same familiar things will not produce different results. To reach new levels of performance, leaders must be prepared to change their behavior, as well as that of others. Second, the research underscored an observation by Jack Welch, former Chairman and CEO of GE: "Before you become a leader, success is all about growing yourself; after you become a leader, success is all about growing others . . ."

thinking to strategy and product positioning, and changing our behavior as a senior team as to how we interact and pursue much clearer defined commercial objectives." Observing the change in one CEO participant, the board chairman of his company had a more dramatic response: "I don't know what's happened to [him]. Six months ago he was talking about selling the company. Now he's talking about rivaling IBM!"

Executive Coaching that Begins and Ends with Business Impact

Executive coaching is yet another leadership development approach that can provide significant benefits when incorporating applied behavioral elements. During the 1980s, executives regarded coaching as the last stop before someone exited the company. By the 1990s, executive coaching had become an activity reserved for senior leaders, often used to quietly tell them that they needed to treat people better.

I personally participated in the coaching initiative because I don't expect my people to do something that I would not do myself. That fundamentally altered the success of the effort. Also, coaching gave me the framework to realize and consider leadership actions that I would not have thought about otherwise.

—SENIOR EXECUTIVE WHO UTILIZED EXECUTIVE COACHING FOR THE TOP 100 LEADERS OF A GLOBAL MERGER INTEGRATION

More recently, coaching trends have bifurcated. Coaching has become commoditized to the point where it seems that nearly everyone is either a coach, being coached, or both. At the same time, coaching has also become the development method of choice for the brightest and best, used to accelerate progress in targeted areas.

Executive coaching can help leaders develop behavioral leadership capability as long as the coaching proceeds according to behavioral principles.

Coaching should focus on measurable business impact. It should also provide feedback on current strengths and gaps in a way that stimulates new insight and commitment to personal behavior change. Ongoing coaching discussions should serve to achieve new knowledge and skills related to behavioral leadership fluency, in addition to providing timely feedback and reinforcement.

Behavior-based executive coaching succeeds when it uses leading and lagging metrics to establish development targets; gauge progress over time; and confirm goal achievement, sustainability, and ROI. Figure 27 provides a starter set of metrics that support most executive coaching needs.

Leadership Team Development While Improving the Business

Building upon the advantages of behavior-based executive coaching for individual leaders, organizations are increasingly utilizing similar approaches for all members of a leadership team, enabling team members to develop a common foundation of behavioral leadership capability, and, even more important, to apply this skillfulness in concert.

Leadership teams rarely request coaching en masse. Rather, a growing number of leadership teams are choosing to invest their leadership development time and budget in acquiring instantly relevant knowledge and skill. Coaching stands as one part of a much larger mix.

Preparing Frontline Supervisors and Managers

Canadian National Railway, BituMine, and other companies profiled here have applied methods for developing behavioral leaders at the front line. Rather than conduct training seminars, they hold two-day working sessions that build a concrete coaching action plan to achieve a BRAVO goal (i.e., the most important, most difficult objective they face).

These working sessions equip managers with the initial knowledge required to pinpoint high-impact behaviors in their work groups, conduct an ABC behavioral analysis of current conditions, and build effective

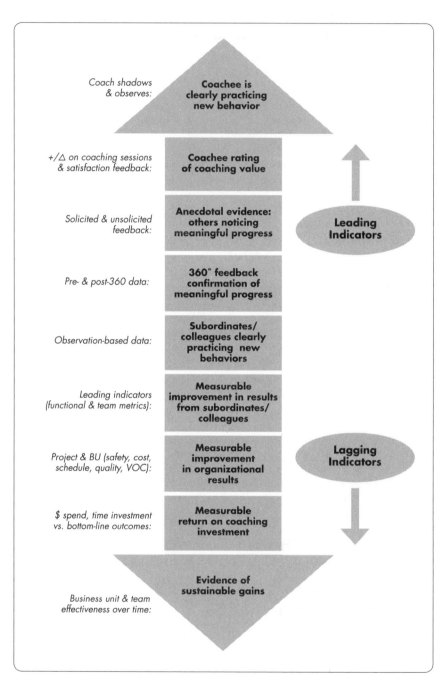

Figure 27. Measuring executive coaching impact

GUIDELINES FOR SELECTING EXECUTIVE COACHING SUPPORT

Proven track record: measurable improvement in leadership effectiveness

Proven track record: measurable business impact from improvements in execution capability

Experience in working with senior executives and high-potential leaders

Experience in working with companies that are similar in size and geographic markets

Sterling reputation, with strong and tangible credentials

Experience in supporting/integrating with other corporate programs and initiatives

Experience in partnering (or providing) with executive-assessment services

Unified best-in-class approach, consistently applied by all coaches

Exemplary, documented process for selecting and developing executive coaches, as well as for ongoing quality assurance

Proven process for providing progress updates across multiple coaching clients (e.g., to HRD, executive team, and/or BOD) while preserving complete confidentiality of individuals

Exemplary customer focus

Highly professional, collaborative working style

Ample capacity

Reasonable price for premium service

Ability and willingness to develop and certify internal executive coaching resources, if desired antecedents, consequences, and leading/lagging progress indicators into their action plans. Also, the working sessions enable managers to understand their own role as consequence providers and to identify the leadership behaviors that will encourage discretionary performance and accelerate behavior change.

Working sessions represent merely the beginning. Companies expect managers to take their action plans and make it happen almost immediately. Moreover, understanding that the working session, no matter how productive, is merely a prompt (an antecedent) for new leadership practices, companies provide a series of one-hour coaching sessions for each manager every few weeks for the next four to six months. The coaching sessions enable each manager to take stock of his or her progress in motivating discretionary performance, determine whether sufficient improvement in target results has occurred, and assess how well he or she has incorporated behavioral leadership practices.

Reflecting upon the impact that this type of development process had on managers, one senior leader in a large health-care company remarked, "We have a manager who rarely went outside her cubicle. She only interacted with her staff if there was a problem. Now she's out there all the time leading cheers for her staff. That team's performance went through the roof! Not only that, the team shows a strong commitment to improvement—all because of the difference in this one manager's communication style. I see the same thing across the board. In the past, if I wanted to go talk to a manager, I just went to their desk. Now, 80 percent of the time, I won't find the managers there. I have to go look for them out on the floor."

TIPS FOR BEHAVIORAL LEADERS

We have so far focused on programs organizations can use to nurture behavioral leadership competencies. How can individual leaders best approach their own development? We offer the following tips.

Tip 1: Set Continuous Improvement Targets for Your Personal Development Goals

Boeing CEO Jim McNerney once related that he sets an annual 15 percent improvement goal for his personal leadership as well as for the leadership of each of his direct reports. Mr. McNerney's example sparked intrigue on the part of a number of leaders as well as a bit of dissonance. As one executive remarked, "I love the idea, but I don't know how to do it." Some executives see leadership as too subjective and intangible to allow for meaningful annual improvement goals.

Behavioral leadership can help here. Behavioral leaders *always* work toward leadership improvement goals, as Mr. McNerney advises. Moreover, they use a simple, repeatable approach for establishing goals and assessing progress. They start with a business outcome they want to improve, clarify the behavior change they need from others, and then link this to improvements they can make in their own practices. All along, they use the four cornerstones of sustainable high performance to prioritize their next leadership improvement targets. Given their business priorities, is it most important that they sharpen their skills in providing Direction, in building new Competence, in ensuring the Opportunity to perform at higher levels, or in Motivating new *discretionary* performance?

As for tracking progress, behavioral leaders use some version of the continuum of leading/lagging indicators in Figure 27. They track how much they actually perform the new practices to which they committed. Soliciting feedback, they learn whether their new behaviors are indeed having the intended effect. They monitor the pace and extent to which they are influencing behavior change in others. And they monitor improvements in targeted business results as lagging indicators of their leadership development.

Tip 2: Practice, Practice, Deliberate Practice

Realizing that they can always become more skillful, strong behavioral leaders accept that ongoing practice is part of success. But not all practice is created equal. Practice that focuses on relatively undeveloped skills works best, even (or, especially) if this means venturing out of your comfort zone.

Execute extremely well and you win. That's why Vince Lombardi, the famous football coach, used to spend eight hours on one sweep. Just one play. Do the simple blocking and tackling and the other stuff will take care of itself. It's the same in . . . business. You get the basics and you'll win.

—DAN HARRINGTON, WORLD SERIES OF POKER CHAMPION

In studying expertise and top performance in areas like surgery, chess, ballet, and sports, researchers have concluded that "outstanding performance is the product of many years of deliberate practice and coaching, not of any innate talent or skill . . . The journey to truly superior performance is neither for the faint of heart nor the impatient . . . The development of genuine expertise requires struggle, sacrifice, and honest, often painful self-assessment . . . Above all, if you want to achieve top performance as a manager and a leader, you've got to forget the folklore about genius that makes many people think they cannot take a scientific approach to developing expertise."[7]

These researchers go on to observe that most people practice skills they have already mastered. "Deliberate practice is different. It entails considerable, specific, and sustained efforts to do something you can't do well—or even at all. Research across a number of domains shows that it is only by working at what you can't do that you turn into the expert you want to become."

• • •

Leadership capability isn't ancillary to the behavior breakthrough—it lies at its very core. This chapter has explored how to develop strong, effective behavioral leaders. We should underscore that developing behavioral leadership capability isn't merely about individual leaders becoming better. It's about learning how to make others great too. Behavioral leaders make the difference in the performance, the careers, and, yes, the lives of those with whom they work. And they do so not merely thanks to generosity and good intentions, but also because of the skill that comes from deliberate practice, feedback, and learning over time.

⟳ *THE BEHAVIORAL LEADER'S SNAPSHOT SUMMARY*

In brief:

- The core capability of behavioral leadership includes the following elements:
  - Behavioral leaders are able to apply the DCOM performance model better than most. Through the organizational processes they establish, as well as the leadership practices that they model, they ensure:
    - Clear direction and alignment throughout the organization
    - Technical and nontechnical competencies
    - The opportunity to perform at sustainably high levels
    - The motivation to contribute discretionary performance
  - They have a strong knowledge of Applied Behavioral Science.
  - They consistently and skillfully demonstrate the Seven Essential Steps of behavioral leadership (chapter 4).

- ○ They effectively apply these skills across the organization to improve annual business plan deployment, coach for elite performance, lead large-scale change, and transform culture for competitive advantage.

- Behavioral leaders develop this capability *while* they are making important things happen.

- They utilize their understanding of the science of behavior to transform leadership development approaches such as executive education, executive coaching, leadership team development, preparing frontline managers, developing high-potential leaders, and even preparing CEOs' success.

- All of these approaches to leadership development begin and end with measurable business impact.

Ask yourself:

☐ How well developed are your behavioral leadership skills and practices? Your leadership team's?

☐ To what extent do your organization's leadership development approaches

- ○ Measure success in terms of business impact?

- ○ Require demonstration of ongoing application and behavior change?

- ○ Provide coaching and reinforcement until new skills and practices are achieved?

☐ Do you establish measurable continuous-improvement objectives for your own leadership practices?

CHAPTER TEN

➲ BUILDING ENTERPRISE ADVANTAGE

Steve Jacobs, Karen Gorman, Vikesh Mahendroo, and Elise Walton

Men stumble over the truth from time to time, but most pick themselves up and hurry off as if nothing happened.
—WINSTON CHURCHILL

Once a company has applied behavioral leadership to accelerate performance in a single operational or administrative area, where can it go from there?

The answer: Wherever leaders can imagine.

Remember that global industrial company profiled in the last chapter? During the mid-to-late 1990s, this organization began to incorporate behavior into every aspect of its business—including strategy, process, and people. The company started by developing behavioral leadership skills in thousands of leaders and managers, with intense focus on the four cornerstones of sustainable high performance (DCOM), effective feedback, and applying the science of behavior (ABCs/E-TIP) to achieve critical objectives.

In just a few short years, the company performed better than ever before. Employee satisfaction rose to unprecedented levels, and the company saw a 40-percent revenue increase. Their behavior breakthrough continues to this day, with sustainable performance gains in every area. "The behavioral approach to our business gives us a huge competitive advantage," said one business-line president. "It's just the way we do business. The results are unmistakable."

The strategies we've presented for achieving an initial behavior break-through are just the beginning. Much as staying in top physical shape requires that an athlete constantly maintain and enhance his training, so achieving sustained advantage requires that companies persist in deliberately fostering the new behaviors they have developed, so that this conduct endures and strengthens. But as we alluded to in chapter 5, the best companies go further still, building capability throughout the enterprise, embedding it in many functions and applying it in myriad ways, nurturing new capability over years in every implementation cycle. A behavioral approach has the potential to change an entire large enterprise, not just one team, product line, or business unit.

Let's now examine in more detail how disciplined organizations can sustain specific behavior changes they've introduced and then broaden their application of the science to gain the fullest long-term advantage possible.

BUILDING HABIT STRENGTH

Though humorous, Winston Churchill's observation that important truths sometimes escape us rings true for organizations. Many companies lack a systematic approach for reinforcing and sustaining behavior change, or "building habit strength," as we call it. They assume that what is now will always be, and so they move on to other priorities and objectives. That's unfortunate, since the science underpinning behavioral leadership has as much to say about *sustaining* behavior change as it does about encouraging new behavior in the first place. The same principles that bring about change can sustain it when continuously applied.

In mobilizing the specific tactics we've shared for making it last, firms should take care to do two basic things. First, *keep moving forward.* Take aim at new results targets. Embrace new high-impact behaviors. Sharpen skillfulness, moving from proficiency to exemplary fluency.

Second, *set the stage for sustainability from the very beginning.* Behavioral leaders work to accomplish certain milestones at each stage of the behavioral execution process. They build in certain activities as they complete MAKE-IT Clear, MAKE-IT Real, and MAKE-IT Happen phases so that the foundation for sustainability is already established as they move on to MAKE-IT Last.

A chemical company sustains change by emphasizing three considerations at each MAKE-IT stage: process and roles, behaviorally based measurement, and effective use of feedback. In MAKE-IT Clear, senior leadership and process owners agree to support behavioralization of business plan deployment and the performance-management process, including their own behaviors. They ensure that they and their leadership teams define success and create leading indicator scorecards. Finally, they confirm that all managers and leaders will gain proficiency as behavioral coaches, implementing a timely, reliable feedback loop with their direct reports.

"This alignment makes the direction—our vision and strategy—very clear from the top to the bottom of the organization," said a business-line manager. "Everyone in the performer chain knows their roles and behaviors—what they should and shouldn't do—to achieve success. This process takes the blame out of the system because everyone knows that each person plays an important role in getting high-quality product out the door without incident, on time, and within budget."

In MAKE-IT Real, leaders look ahead and prioritize the processes (onboarding, development, promotion, etc.) the company will need to sustain behavioral improvements. Building upon MAKE-IT Clear, leaders design and disseminate a success story framework to further clarify the end goal; they also decide upon the data, anecdotes, and learning that will document progress along the way.

This practice is valuable not merely for the alignment and shared vision it yields, but for the clarity that comes with putting words and numbers onto the page. During this phase, as each level of leadership is charged with now doing something new, managers establish feedback loops with direct reports and put mechanisms in place that enable senior sponsors to experience changes that are beginning to crop up.

"Giving constructive feedback was very difficult for us when we started," reported a technology-center leader in a product-manufacturing company. "We have a culture where everyone is really nice and we don't say anything that might hurt someone's feelings. Once we learned how to give feedback with the intent of helping people do things better, it was much easier. The feedback tracking system also made it obvious if we were giving too much or too little feedback to any one individual, which helped us be fair—another important cultural attribute."

In MAKE-IT Happen, managers consider whom to hold accountable for ensuring needed process realignments. They hold routine feedback meetings to review leading indicators, document success stories with relevant data, and capture key learnings. They also analyze setbacks to determine if the challenges owe to flaws in strategy or execution. Two-way feedback discussions routinely take place between managers and their direct reports at each level to ensure consistent learning, meaningful encouragement, and timely corrections wherever appropriate.

In MAKE-IT Last, managers establish clear accountability for sustainability of results and behavioral changes. This includes singular accountability for sustaining and continuously improving the behavioral leadership capability acquired in the current implementation cycle. Sustainability metrics are confirmed, and sustainability workshops are conducted to reinforce key learnings and confirm sustainability actions and accountabilities going forward. Periodic sustainability audits are conducted. Frequently, behavioral leaders will also conduct advanced coaching labs to equip managers and leaders with specific coaching tools and practices that help keep habits strong and vital.

We cannot emphasize enough the importance of protecting against gradual dilution of your hard-won gains! Behavioral leadership is a distinct and powerful lever for performance and applies broadly to a range of strategic imperatives. Initial success does not guarantee your continued success, any more than reaching a new level of physical conditioning guarantees that you will continue your progress as an athlete. Managers must pay constant attention to embed the capability in the organization's DNA. Sooner or later, the sponsors who initially grasped the behavioral leadership opportunity and who led the early progress will move on. And then what?

Companies that have led the way in sustainability practices anticipate leadership transitions, plan for them, and leverage them to the fullest. These companies build commitment at the organization's highest levels, often including the board of directors, by the second year of deployment. They also build as much business-as-usual durability in practices and processes as possible.

When the time comes to manage the transition from one leader to another, these companies then make sure to address each of the DCOM success factors. They clearly identify behavioral leadership capability and desired culture as priorities for the organization and as selection criteria for the open leadership position. In fact, some companies are beginning to use assessment processes in their hiring that are specifically designed to ensure the selection of the Q4 Leadership attributes that we discussed in chapter 4.

Once selected, new leaders receive briefings on behavior-based applications, results, and learning from past implementation cycles as well as on implications for their own leadership practices. Within the first ninety days, the new leader participates in behavioral-leadership skill development processes as part of on-boarding, establishes clear enhancement targets for his or her own practices, and verifies that he or she possesses effective sources of feedback and has progress metrics in place. Dashboard metrics in the organization's management reports monitor ongoing progress in sustaining and leveraging behavioral-leadership application cycles. In sum, the company does not leave continuity to chance. It is a priority and managed as such.

BEYOND SUSTAINABILITY: BUILDING ENTERPRISE ADVANTAGE

Once a company has sustained behavior change in an area, leaders can feel tempted to rest on their laurels and forgo further change. The best behavioral leaders view initial accomplishments as the reason to stay the course, broaden and deepen their behavioral leadership acumen, and drive to a more formidable position (see Figure 28).

Ultimately, they seek the kind of enterprise advantage that can only be achieved through continuity, ingenuity, and persistence. And they build

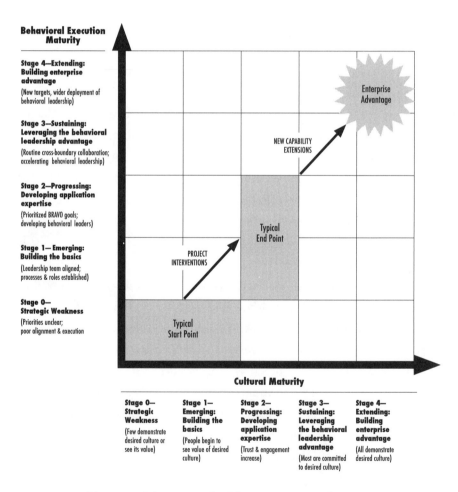

Figure 28. The steps to building enterprise advantage

this enterprise advantage by extending to new areas and audiences, targeting new types of performance results (and therefore new types of behavior), integrating new implications for formal organizational processes, developing more advanced "201-level" sophistication in applying the science, and incorporating new deployment tactics. Let's examine some of these elements in turn.

New Areas and Audiences

For most organizations, implementation of behavioral leadership typically occurs first within a single business unit. From there, initial adopters move to their next cycles of application (e.g., by aiming at a new move-the-needle objective), while new groups commence adoption, both within the first business unit and in new units and functions.

As we've seen, the Bank of Montreal first developed and applied behavioral leadership capabilities across 250 managers within one division. Based upon results from this initial implementation cycle, BMO's leadership elected to extend this capability coast to coast across the remaining 1,000 leaders in that unit. They then applied this embedded base of capability beyond operational performance and consumer loyalty to accelerate execution of large-scale change initiatives.

Boards of directors are increasingly adopting behavioral approaches to improve their governance. The chair of the governance committee of a large, notable—and notably misaligned—board of directors correctly observed that most of the board's challenges really owed to unproductive behavior. He also noted that, despite the board's laudable efforts to document and implement its charter, committee structure, roles, and accountabilities, it had not occurred to the directors to define behaviors expected of all board members. By agreeing on pinpointed behavioral principles, the board set itself on a new path for more productive governance.

New Types of Performance Results (and New High-Impact Behavior)

Behavioral leadership is especially exciting for its versatility and applicability across a wide spectrum of performance challenges. Let's look at some of the applications companies can incorporate over time.

New Annual Plan Priorities

Chapter 5 discussed the process for reassessing which strategic priorities most merit application of an organization's growing behavioral execution capability. We note here that such BRAVO goals, as we call them, do not necessarily need to all be operational breakthroughs. Increasingly, they can target results that at first glance seem unrelated or impervious to behavior change:

- Rather than driving sales growth through traditional sales improvement levers (such as firing/hiring, sales training, CRM upgrades, and sales compensation adjustments), experienced companies might shape desired sales behavior consistently across the field sales force.

- Similarly, with spiraling US health-care costs threatening the global competitiveness of a number of companies, behavioral leaders are increasingly focusing their capability on annual improvements in healthy behaviors and related health-care cost control.

- Still other companies are recognizing the central role that behavior plays in achieving innovation objectives, assigning BRAVO goals accordingly.

In the early 2000s, we worked with a global biologics company with a long history of industry-leading innovation. Their leaders wanted to make sure the work environment allowed innovation to continue flourishing. They understood from our early research and alignment sessions that leadership behaviors (like providing time to focus on innovation, accepting mistakes when employees tried something new, giving people decision-making authority, and rewarding contributions) could both enhance and limit employees' creativity, ideation, and problem solving. As a result of their learning, leaders throughout the R&D organization adopted and embedded new behaviors in their strategies, processes, and programs that drove, recognized, nurtured, and rewarded innovation. Today, this company is a leading developer of first-to-market life-saving drugs.

High-Impact Decisions

Most organizations make a small number of big-bet decisions in a given year (e.g., concerning capital allocation or financial forecasting). Behavioral leaders rightly view such decision making as a special class of behavior, namely (a) high-impact behavior that (b) occurs infrequently in which (c) a small number of senior leader performers must (d) perform together to make decisions in which (e) the stakes for the organization are significant and perhaps enormous, and where (f) the feedback loops are protracted across years before the quality of the decision is known.

To make such decisions well, leaders must combine three types of high-impact behavior: preparation for decision-making meetings, facilitation of meetings using a rigorous agenda, and basing decisions on data (versus best estimate or opinion). While such behaviors may sound mundane, a behavioral approach to high-impact group decision making drives very different practices in most companies and yields profoundly different outcomes.

Multiyear Project Yield

Companies in industries ranging from pharmaceuticals to global oil, microprocessor manufacturing to commercial real estate, all struggle to obtain the greatest yield possible from long-term capital projects. Most by necessity maintain relatively effective control processes for monitoring on-time/on-budget performance.

Behavioral leaders go further. Recognizing that every month is an opportunity to save or lose millions in the project budget—and that day-to-day behavior plays a big role in preventing costly surprises, rework, and give-backs due to performance variances—such leaders identify and shape high-impact behavior at every stage of the project, starting on month one.

The project director of a five-year joint-venture development project in the Middle East quickly recognized that the individual leadership behavior of members of his senior leadership team was proving counterproductive in the field. While the impact would not surface for some time, he calculated an opportunity cost of three to five months across the sixty-month project, valued at $50 million per month. This was sufficient reason for senior team members to agree in unison on their year-one high-impact behaviors and, with coaching support, to lead greater alignment in the field.

Cross-Boundary Collaboration

Nearly every organization talks about the need to "break down walls" and "bust silos." In fact, more than 97 percent of senior leaders believe collaboration is essential to business success.[1] Unfortunately, companies usually don't improve collaboration. Moreover, leaders in many organizations are perceived to lack the skills necessary to develop meaningful collaboration. Only 47 percent of senior leaders, and notably only 30 percent of employees, rate leaders in their organizations as skilled in collaboration.[2]

Collaboration is behavior, and improved collaboration requires behavior change. Behavioral leaders do two unusual things to foster collaboration. First, they take care to gain agreement on *where* throughout the organization collaboration adds most value to customers, employees, and shareholders. They link collaboration directly to results. Out of the many cross-boundary interdependencies across an enterprise, they build alignment around those few that matter most. Second—you guessed it—they pinpoint the necessary high-impact collaborative behavior, and then set about encouraging it.

When a pharmaceutical company decided to outsource a portion of its clinical trials, stakeholders from both sides recognized collaboration at the point of handoff as one of the most critical behaviors. For the company's employees the question was, "Can I trust them to do it as well as we did and achieve our high performance standards?" The out-sourcer's concern was, "Will they be able to let go so we can do our jobs and meet their needs?"

The high-impact collaborative behaviors that the teams agreed to per-form, and to coach one another on, were: checking assumptions about their partners at the door and assuming positive intent, openly and quickly acknowledging mistakes and risks to performance, jointly agree-ing on plans to address problems, and providing feedback about what is and isn't working well.

In yet another example, a global professional-services firm saw collab-orative consulting across three separate global entities as an opportunity to serve clients better and generate new revenue. But the three entities had separate P&Ls, different incentive plans, and different performance man-agement systems, so nothing incentivized managers to seek collaborative revenue. Further, some saw such revenue as double counting.

The leader over the three entities saw genuine benefits and chartered a cross-company steering group. He assigned a senior executive to lead the initiative. The priority appeared on meeting agendas, revenue was reported in quarterly updates to the parent company, and some group members modeled joint sales and prospect calls.

The group educated consultants and management teams on the collab-oration process and how to team for client visits. They identified intrinsi-cally collaborative consultants to lead early projects and highlighted early successes in meetings. Team members determined incentive-plan credits to avoid disputes. Incentive awards went to managers of recipients after regular bonuses were calculated in order to ensure that those who dem-onstrated the cross-selling performance indeed received the full awards.

Over three years, incremental annual revenue reached $40 million. Incentive awards, recognition at company meetings, and newsletter arti-cles reinforced the behavior. Managers came to enjoy handing out sub-stantial collaboration awards. Satisfied clients attested to the value they received, and the firm managed to keep some competitors at bay. Using behavioral leadership principles, the company achieved cross-selling performance (which is notoriously difficult to motivate) by carefully realigning the balance of consequences for success.

Light-Touch Behavior Change

Behavioral leadership can facilitate not merely difficult behavior change, but "light-touch" enhancement of desired behavior that is already taking place. For instance, employee behavior such as consistently turning off computers and desktop equipment at the end of the day can significantly impact energy conservation and energy costs. Is this a relatively easy behavior to perform? Certainly. Is it likely to happen consistently and sustainably across hundreds or thousands of employees? Not at all.

In reinforcing such habits, behavioral leaders learn to skillfully match level of intensity with level of need. Rather than applying a pound of cure (e.g., systematic coaching for elite performance) when an ounce will do, experienced companies might simply ensure that managers are spending five minutes twice monthly in team meetings holding data-based, reinforcement-based dialogues around progress to date in their work group.

New Implications for Organizational Processes

Behavioral leaders who successfully extend their capability throughout the enterprise evolve a number of organizational processes to support this purpose. In many cases, the changes represent relatively small shifts that, once understood, are relatively easy to adopt. They can lead to powerfully different outcomes.

For example, behavioral leaders typically realign these things: their values statement, metrics, business excellence processes, project management and monitoring processes, core business processes including new-product development and service delivery, selection and on-boarding, training and development, strategic talent management, performance management and promotion, and compensation/recognition.

More Advanced "201" Sophistication in Applying the Science

Many of the leaders we've worked with appreciate how much always remains to be learned, even with early successes, and how much additional advantage comes with additional effort. As Tony McGuire, CEO of System Dynamics, once remarked, "Every time I think I've got it all, I learn another piece that adds more value to what we're doing. Surprisingly, this makes me hungry for more."

More Powerful Antecedents

Increased sophistication and savvy with behavior often enables leaders to deploy more powerful antecedents. Consequences typically have greater power than antecedents (remember the 80/20 impact of consequences and antecedents), but antecedents remain important because they prompt new behavior.

One company realized that in holding an annual Top 300 leadership conference they were essentially making a sizable expenditure on an antecedent. Rather than eliminate the event, they leveraged it much more deliberately as an investment and, more specifically, as a powerful trigger for accelerating specific behavior changes that leaders wanted to encourage.

This shift in orientation led to a number of new practices. Rather than simply designing the event, meeting planners now begin by confirming the "know, feel, and *do*" objectives with the executive team, deriving the "do" objectives from previously established high-impact, culture-building, and BRAVO goal behaviors.

Meeting planners specifically identify expected actions for the Top 300 leaders one week, one month, and three months after the meeting, and they develop presentations and working sessions with these behavioral objectives in mind. The day before the meeting, forty senior officers meet to confirm how they will serve as consequence providers, both during and after the event.

You can imagine how much higher the yield is from this company's meeting, given the much clearer focus.

More Powerful Consequences

As we've seen, leadership practices can serve as effectively encouraging or discouraging consequences that are also relatively inexpensive to provide. That said, the Pyramid of Consequences discussed in chapters 3 and 7 reminds us that behavioral leaders have additional, and very influential, sources of consequences available to them. With experience, peer and social sources of consequences, self-based sources of reinforcement, and natural consequences come to serve as powerful supplements to organizational and leadership levers.

New Deployment Tactics

A final dimension of building enterprise capability consists of enhancing deployment tactics. In their initial implementation cycles, companies might establish the foundation for accelerated "pull" by deliberately focusing behavior-based activities on improvements that boost the business *and* leave managers and employees marveling that "we've not been able to accomplish this in the past."

Companies might also choose leaders and managers in the initial cycles based in part on the respect they garner from others; that way, team members will listen when these managers describe in positive, first-person terms, "what's new and different" in the approach.

Companies can combine rigorous measurement (enabling leaders to speak factually and empirically) with anecdotes and stories that convey the emotional benefits people are experiencing. Ian, a regional vice president of operations, summarized for enterprise officers and peers what he had learned as a senior sponsor of behavioral leadership demonstration projects. He spoke from objective data calmly and effectively, describing how a number of operational indicators had improved over the past six months, including breakthroughs in customer-first performance.

Then Ian turned off the projection device and said, "But . . . that's not the real story. The real story is . . . "

Ian couldn't finish his sentence; he choked up. He paused for a moment to regain his composure. "The real story is culture."

Ian went on to explain that the groups involved, including union employees, had long conflicted with one another. People whose offices were fifty feet from one another went weeks communicating via email, if at all, so they didn't have to speak to one another. They protected long-standing procedures that effectively masked the problems customers were experiencing.

In just a few months, acrimony and entitlement had yielded to collaboration and initiative. While the numbers made the case for behavioral leadership, Ian wanted the group to know that the magnitude of what had been accomplished went beyond the numbers. Indeed, he said, it was "beyond words."

Experienced companies can also grow their capability across the enterprise by thoughtfully locating their extensions and the leaders of those initiatives. Companies don't have to seed the entire enterprise landscape all at once. By inserting the right initiatives in the right locations and then redeploying proven behavioral leaders, leaders can enable desired behaviors to take root over time across the rest of the organization.

MAKING IT BUSINESS AS USUAL

We've cataloged the ways that companies can deploy a behavioral approach throughout an entire organization, but what does it look like when full enterprise capability exists? Simply put, behavioral competency doesn't stand out so much day-to-day, because it has become a constant and abiding presence within what has become a high-performing, industry-leading organization.

Let's return to the global industrial company described at the beginning of this chapter. The day was just starting in one part of the world and had already ended in another when twenty-five of the global business unit's top leaders from four points around the earth gathered on a teleconference to discuss improving safety performance.

In launching this effort, the president attributed improvements over the previous seven years to two major items: strong management and leadership commitment to excellent safety performance, and significant use of performance-based safety to shift the safety culture around the world from "compliance" to a belief that accidents can be avoided. The improvement process, however, appeared to have run out of steam—and that needed to change.

"Let's start with a DCOM analysis," a leader suggested. The *Direction* was clear: Everyone knew that safety was the company's top priority and that the metrics on safety performance were well communicated and visible in all work locations. There were no gaps on *Competence*, either; every employee received extensive safety training before and during the job and safety briefings before beginning any task. The leaders also agreed that people had the *Opportunity* to work safely, even to the point of having permission to stop work if something wasn't safe. Concluding that the problem was a *Motivation* issue, the group decided to conduct an ABC analysis to determine why employees were not behaving as desired.

The assessment proved their hypothesis and revealed that the consequences experienced by employees were encouraging different behaviors than desired. Fear of losing their jobs and the perceived need to protect their coworkers were inhibiting employees from reporting minor incidents. Employees also cited complicated procedures that led to procedural noncompliance because it was easier and faster to do the work another way, even if it wasn't as safe. Finally, while everyone acknowledged safety as the top priority, they experienced significant discouragement regarding schedule and budget adherence, driving the occasional corner cutting that increased incident risk. Employees also reported receiving very little, if any, positive or constructive feedback about safe behaviors from anyone.

With input from all parts of the organization around the world, the leaders spotlighted consequence management and effective feedback as the key factors to improving safety performance. What resonated most with the workforce at all levels was the responsibility each individual accepted to *provide positive and constructive feedback to ensure his/her own and others' safety.* It was as simple as saying to a coworker, "Thanks for checking my harness to make sure I had it on right." Within months, key performance indicators trended in the right direction, and by year-end the business unit had exceeded its goals.

Stories like this abound in this corporation; it's the way they do business from top to bottom. No matter where you go in the world or what language employees speak, day in and day out they all understand *and apply* behavioral leadership and its associated tools, like DCOM, ABCs, consequence management, and feedback. Behavioral leadership is ingrained in their culture and is now the language of their business—valid indication of enterprise capability.

THE BEHAVIORAL LEADERSHIP ADVANTAGE (OR, THE FIRST MOVER ADVANTAGE)

Companies that make the greatest, most sustained effort at achieving an enterprise capability usually keep pretty quiet about it. The chairman of a Fortune 50 company explained why at an annual industry conference: "What we are doing on the people side is where our company's real success will come from. This is how we are going to make a real difference in our performance as an organization. It is one of the most exciting things I've ever been part of. But I'm not going to tell you about it! The reason is because we believe it is our company's secret weapon." He and his organization had not only discovered the power of the behavior breakthrough—achieving competitive advantage through behavioral leadership—but also planned to *extend* this advantage in coming years.

This leader made his remarks more than a decade ago. As of this writing, two CEO successions later, the company is still developing and leveraging behavioral leadership in many forms for marketplace advantage. The organization's leaders have used behavioral leadership to achieve performance breakthroughs in business unit after business unit, in facility after facility, on continent after continent.

Top leaders have certified nearly three hundred executives worldwide in behaviorally based decision-making processes to improve the yield of capital decisions. They have behavioralized annual plan prioritization and deployment in key divisions, achieving significant gains in a range of operational performance metrics including plant reliability, safety, productivity, quality, environmental compliance, logistics efficiencies, and cost management. They have made coaching for elite performance a way of life in many parts of the company and have integrated behavioral methods into their process improvement and change management methodologies, enhancing everything from technology implementations to merger integrations. As one might expect, they have transformed their organizational culture along the way as well.

Has the company reaped a financial reward? And how! Profit increases are now in the billions of dollars. And the company has significantly advanced its position in the Fortune 50 rankings. Neither we nor the company's leadership would attribute all of this to a behavioral approach. Yet behavioral leadership has played an indisputable role in this success, comprising a distinct source of advantage.

Leading the Revolution

This organization is one of a select and growing group of companies that is leading the "quiet revolution." Twenty years in the making, behavioral leadership is now well established in its ability to drive superior execution. As we related in chapter 1, seizing this advantage begins with having "new eyes" that recognize the powerful connection between new behavior and new results as well as the practical utility of harnessing the science of behavior.

As a leader within your organization, ask yourself: "Is applying behavioral leadership capability smart business for us? If so, where do we go from here?" In answering these questions, consider, too, the following:

- What are my critical business challenges?

- Does success require people to do new things, and then continue to do these things, exhibiting sustained behavior change?

- If so, how can I begin building behavioral leadership capability within my organization?

  o Where do I start? Where are greenhouse applications both vital and fertile?

  o How do I ensure that we establish the right conditions for initial success?

  o How do I protect against distractions and unnecessary impediments?

- How do I ensure that the efforts I make remain as our legacy?

  o How do I ensure that the right knowledge transfer takes place?

- How do I embed the capability toward the areas that will give us ongoing lift? For instance, how will I embed the capability toward our strategy for:

  o Customer retention?

  o Customer growth?

  o Global expansion?

  o Toughing it out during the uncertain economic climate?

  o Mergers and acquisitions?

  o New product development?

- How do I elevate the visibility of this powerful tool?

Knowing about behavior is important, but as we've also said repeatedly throughout this book, it isn't the same as doing. What distinguishes behavioral leaders is an unrelenting pursuit of broader, deeper application every cycle, every year. The German poet Goethe once observed: "What you have inherited from your fathers, you must earn in order to possess."

Indeed, pioneers in behavioral leadership have recognized perhaps the greatest advantage that the approach affords: *Competitors cannot purchase it off the shelf. They cannot reverse engineer it. They cannot imitate it overnight. There are no shortcuts.*

Skillful behavioral leaders can learn from those who have gone before them and, in fact, that's why we have written *The Behavior Breakthrough.* But companies can only possess competitive advantage by earning it through repeated experience. Those who have a head start will more likely maintain that advantage for many years to come.

Here's to getting started.

⮑ EPILOGUE

Try not to become a man of success but rather to become a man of value.

—ALBERT EINSTEIN

We began *The Behavior Breakthrough* with a simple premise: New results require new behavior. Understanding how to apply the science of behavior change can create a formidable new advantage for companies that choose to build this execution capability. We have described the methods that behavioral leaders use to build and leverage this capability, as well as seven principles that guide them:

1. Superior execution drives competitive advantage, and skillful behavior change drives superior execution.

2. Leading skillful behavior change requires experienced application of the science.

3. Peak performance requires *discretionary* performance.

4. Discretionary performance requires a positive work culture and positive leadership practices.

5. Build for sustainability and habit strength at every stage of deployment.

6. Develop behavioral leaders while they are making important things happen.

7. Build new enterprise capability in every implementation cycle.

THE EIGHTH PRINCIPLE: CARE

Years ago, Leslie Braksick, our colleague and CLG cofounder, was asked to describe our approach to bringing the science of behavior to business. Leslie's response was profound in its simplicity: "Care. Really care. Show you care." This principle has served us at CLG very well over the years. In fact, when our clients say that we are "different from the rest," they are as likely to be referring to *how we work with them* as they are about the behavioral leadership expertise that we bring.

Reflecting upon the last two decades of our experience, there is a lesson here for all of us. Behavioral leadership is not just about knowing the science or using the tools. It's not just about methods. To be extraordinary, behavioral leaders must care about those with whom they work. Really care. And show they care.

WHAT'S IN IT FOR YOU?

Throughout *The Behavior Breakthrough*, we have emphasized the benefits of behavioral leadership for your organization, for your employees, and even for your customers and suppliers. But what about you? As a leader, what are the implications for you? Developing skillful behavioral leadership practices takes time and effort. Is it really worth it?

We asked Dave Moran, President and CEO of Heinz Europe, for his view. Dave has successfully applied behavioral leadership capability in three major assignments in the last decade, and he speaks from personal experience:

> I have a simple answer for any leader who is seriously considering behavioral leadership as an approach. Do it. It's easier work, not harder. You're more effective. And, you sleep better at night.
>
> Behavioral leadership definitely requires developing some practices that are different from what many of us learn in our normal career development. But that doesn't mean that it's harder work. It

really is easier, once you build the foundation. You have greater clarity on what observable behavior matters most, why current behavior is occurring, and what your best levers are for motivating behavior change. You're able to speak objectively and dispassionately to people about things they need to improve. And, you're balancing this with frequent encouragement that you know is meaningful to your people and that helps to move the ball down the field.

Second, you know you're more effective because you routinely see things that would never have occurred previously. Despite the common belief that "people don't change," people *do* change how they act when you're leading with behavioral methods. I routinely see transformations in individuals and leadership teams that, honestly, I would previously have thought "no way" was it possible.

Finally, you sleep better at night because you know that you've done everything there is to do to set clear expectations for both results *and* behavior, to provide ongoing feedback so people know where they stand and what they can do to improve, to clear the deck of obstacles, and to provide consistent support and encouragement. You know that, under these circumstances, most people will rise to the occasion and excel. And when they don't, you know that you've provided every reasonable opportunity for them to succeed.

What I would share with other leaders is that behavioral leadership shouldn't be confused with a "soft" management style. Being clear, dispassionate, objective and fair, firm and yet affirming, is not soft. It's smart business. And it's the right thing to do because you are making a positive difference in people's work lives.

Perhaps the most important lesson that the science behind behavioral leadership teaches us is that, whether we know it or not, we are making a difference in others' work lives every day. Helen Keller once remarked, "The best and most beautiful things in the world cannot be seen or even touched. They must be felt with the heart."

What we reinforce or discourage, intentionally or quite unintentionally, makes a difference. A difference that others feel. The question is, "Is it the right difference? Is it the difference that you want to be remembered by?" So, choose well the difference that you want to make in the workplace. And may the principles of behavioral leadership serve along the way.

We wish you the best of luck!

NOTES

Chapter Two: Your Return on Revolution

1. The authors wish to thank Pam Monahan for her thorough review and comments regarding key results that are summarized in this chapter.

2. CEO, Springfield ReManufacturing Corporation, and author, *The Great Game of Business* (New York: Currency/Doubleday, 1994).

3. The actual correlation coefficient was $r = .80$, $p < .001$, a substantial finding, especially given norms in the social sciences.

4. A. Guiffrida and R. Nagi, "Economics of Managerial Neglect in Supply Chain Delivery Performance," *The Engineering Economist* (2006), 51:1–17.

Chapter Three: Drivers of Sustainable High Performance

1. In addition to the company task force, three other major companies from different industries conducted similar investigations during this period. The four dimensions of sustained high performance were supported by each of the independent corporate initiatives.

2. We have drawn upon the following sources for the hospital physician hand washing example in this section: "Wash your hands," *Harvard Men's Health Watch,* July, 2006, pp. 5–6; Atul Gawande, *Better: A Surgeon's Notes on Performance* (New York: Picador, 2007), pp. 13–28).

Chapter Four: Putting Behavioral Leadership into Practice—Seven Essential Steps

1. S. Keller, "How to Get Senior Leaders to Change," HBR Blog Network, June 14, 2012.

2. R. Blake and J. Mouton, *The Managerial Grid: The Key to Leadership Excellence* (Houston: Gulf Publishing, 1964).

Chapter Six: Coaching for Elite Performance

1. "Violin Virtuoso Roman Totenberg Dies at 101," National Public Radio, *Morning Edition*, May 9, 2012, http://www.npr.org/2012/05/09/152319306/violin-virtuoso-roman-totenberg-dies-at-101

2. 2002 study by Mercer Human Resource Consulting, reported in L.J. Adrianse, "Managing Performance Every Day," http://ezinearticles.com/?Managing-Performance-Every-Day&id=15478. In another study, A.D. Smet, et al., report that, across a number of industries, managers devote only 10 to 40 percent of their time managing frontline employees, of which coaching is only one fraction. "Unlocking the Potential of Frontline Managers," *McKinsey Quarterly,* August 2009, p. 3.

3. See Leslie Braksick's book, *Unlock Behavior, Unleash Profits* (New York: McGraw-Hill, 2007) for a more complete description of how the science of behavior underpins the IMPACT coaching process.

Chapter Seven: Changing the Way Organizations Change

1. G.R. Sullivan and M.V. Harper, *Hope Is Not a Method* (New York: Broadway, 1997), p. xvii.

2. William R. Johnson, *Preparing CEOs for Success* (Pittsburgh: H. J. Heinz, 2010), p. 190.

3. Linda Barrington, "CEO Challenges 2010," Conference Board, February 2010.

Chapter Eight: Winning on Culture

1. "Culture eats strategy for breakfast" is a remark attributed to Peter Drucker and popularized in 2006 by Mark Fields, president of Ford Motor Company, where it continues to hang in the company's war room. As the leader of Ford, Fields was keenly aware that no matter how far-reaching his vision or how brilliant his strategy, neither would be realized if it was not supported by the culture. See http://www.relationaldynamicsinstitute.com/?p=48. Also referenced by Dr. Charles O'Reilly's important work in the area of culture and culture change.

2. See M. Parker, *The Culture Connection* (New York: McGraw-Hill, 2012). See also J.R. Katzenbach, et al., "Culture Change That Sticks," *Harvard Business Review*, July–August 2012, pp. 110–117.

3. J. Johnson, L. Dakens, P. Edwards, and N. Morse, *SwitchPoints: Culture Change on the Fast Track to Business Success* (New York: Wiley, 2008), chapter 2.

4. D. Boorstin, *The Discoverers: A History of Man's Search to Know His World and Himself* (Vintage, 1983), p. 647.

5. Merriam-Webster defines culture as "the set of shared attitudes, values, goals, and practices that characterizes an institution or organization; for example, a corporate culture focused on the bottom line" (http://www.merriam-webster.com/dictionary/culture). Ravasi and Schultz (2006) state that organizational culture is a set of shared mental assumptions that guide interpretation and action in organizations by defining appropriate behavior for various situations (D. Ravasi and M. Schultz, "Responding to Organizational Identity Threats: Exploring the Role of Organizational Culture," *Academy of Management Journal* 49:3, June 1, 2006, pp. 433–458). Businessdictionary.com defines organizational culture as "the values and behaviors that contribute to the unique social and psychological environment of an organization" (http://www.businessdictionary.com/definition/organizational-culture.html).

In a review of business school concepts, Steven Silbiger shares the commonly accepted definition that "culture is the aggregate of behaviors, thoughts, beliefs, and symbols that are conveyed to people throughout an organization over time" (*The Ten Day MBA*, 3rd edition, referencing the "style" component in the 7-S model from Tom Peters).

6. J. Johnson, et al., *SwitchPoints: Culture Change on the Fast Track to Business Success* (New York: Wiley, 2008), pp. 191–192.

7. See L. Dakens, *Employee Performance Scorecards: Creating a Win-Win Formula for Your Organization* (New York: Thomson Reuters, 2009).

8. J. Collins, *Good to Great: Why Some Companies Make the Leap . . . And Others Don't* (New York: HarperCollins, 2001).

9. M. Tushman and C. O'Reilly III, *Winning Through Innovation: A Practical Guide to Leading Organizational Change and Renewal* (Boston: Harvard Business School Press, 1997, 2002), p. 35.

10. N. Nohria, W. Joyce, and B. Roberson, "What Really Works," *Harvard Business Review,* July 2003, p. 47.

Chapter Nine: Developing Behavioral Leaders

1. "Voice of the Leader: Quantitative Analysis of Leadership Bench Strength Development Strategies" (Corporate Leadership Council, 2001).

2. R. J. Kramer, "Have We Learned Anything about Leadership Development?" *The Conference Board Review,* May/June 2008; M. Higgs, "What Do We Really Know about Effective Leadership in Change Management?" The Conference Board Executive Action Series, January 2006.

3. To be clear on this point, the average ratings of leaders' honesty and integrity by both groups are high overall. The point here is simply that there is a statistically significant difference in the extent

to which leaders rated their honesty and integrity higher than did their direct reports.

4. This questioning took place as part of a study later published in in book form by Braksick and Hillgren: *Preparing CEOs for Success: What I Wish I Knew* (Pittsburgh: H.J. Heinz, 2010).

5. P. Chadwick and R. Millar, "Exploring the Executive Development Ecosystem," *Developing Leaders*, Issue 4, 2011, p. 15.

6. To date, nearly 200 CEOs and their companies have participated in one of eight cycles of the program across three sectors (four IT sector programs supported by Stanford Graduate School of Business; two construction and engineering sector programs supported by Duke Corporate Education; and two food sector programs supported by Switzerland's International Institute for Management Development).

7. K. A. Ericsson, M. J. Prietula, and E. T. Cokely, "The Making of an Expert," *Harvard Business Review*, July 2007.

Chapter Ten: Building Enterprise Advantage

1. A. Martin, *What's Next? The 2007 Changing Nature of Leadership Survey*, a Center for Creative Leadership research white paper.

2. M. Scurrah, "The Role of Collaboration in Organizations," October 2008, http://ezinearticles.com/?The-Role-of-Collaboration-in-Organizations&id=1571695

BEHAVIOR BREAKTHROUGH COAUTHORS

Steve Jacobs, MA, Chairman and Senior Partner
Steve Jacobs is highly regarded for his insightful work with senior executives in achieving new performance, culture change, and lasting competitive advantage across a wide range of enterprises. Clients trust his quality leadership, coaching, and implementation strategies and his counsel is sought by Fortune 100 corporate leaders. He speaks frequently at corporate and conference events. Steve holds an interdisciplinary BA from the University of California and a master's degree from Harvard University.

Carolina Aguilera, PhD, CLG Principal
Carolina Aguilera is noted for establishing a quick rapport while winning the trust and confidence of an organization at all levels. A versatile coach, she helps top leaders in the United States, Europe, and Latin America achieve desired results, and her remarkable abilities in team development and change management help successfully execute cultural transformations. Carolina holds a PhD in Psychology (Behavior Analysis) from West Virginia University.

Leslie W. Braksick, PhD, CLG Cofounder
Leslie W. Braksick is a veteran CEO coach, entrepreneur, consultant, author, keynote speaker, and board member. A former CEO herself—who knows the territory intimately—she is a resource often tapped by top executives and boards of Fortune 100 companies to provide coaching support, insight, and executive advising. She holds a doctorate in Applied Behavioral Science from Western Michigan University and an MPH from Johns Hopkins University.

Karen M. Bush, PhD, Senior Principal

Karen Bush expertly applies Applied Behavioral Science (ABS) to align her Fortune 100 clients around goals and achieve results through behavior change. Her diverse background in deploying corporate initiatives and integrating ABS into the annual business cycle, and her ability to relate to and support managers who are undergoing transitions, both place her in high demand. Karen holds an MS and PhD in Experimental Behavior Analysis from the University of Pittsburgh.

Paula Butte, MBA, CLG Partner

Paula Butte is a talented consultant and performance coach recognized by Fortune 500 clients for her business insight, strategy execution expertise, and talent for building internal coaching capabilities. Drawing from extensive marketing and operations management experience, she has a track record of successfully helping leaders create and sustain culture change and receive maximum returns for their consulting investment. She earned her MBA from Central Michigan University.

Kathy Callahan, CLG Partner

Kathy Callahan brings a unique combination of business and consulting experience to companies seeking her practical, real-world solutions. Sought for her work with leadership teams and an expert in large-scale organizational change initiatives, she has assisted numerous Fortune 100 companies with improving their performance. Kathy previously worked in commercial roles for fourteen years in the petrochemicals industry and holds a degree in Chemistry from Duke University.

Charles Carnes, MA, CLG Senior Partner

Charles Carnes is respected for his intellect, professionalism, and energy. He specializes in coaching senior leaders to produce measurably superior and sustainable results while helping them identify the complex cause-and-effect relationships driving business performance. An Associate Certified Coach with the International Coach Federation, he is an expert at self-assessments, 360° feedback, observation, and coaching. Charles earned an MA in Industrial and Organizational Psychology from the University of North Carolina at Charlotte.

Brian Cole, PhD, CLG Principal

Brian Cole has more than fifteen years of coaching and consulting experience, aligning behavior to results and helping leaders create a work environment where employee engagement and discretionary performance become "business as usual." He is known for his special talent for working with senior leaders to build strong teams and produce quantifiable improvements in management effectiveness. Brian holds a PhD in Industrial/Organizational Psychology from Auburn University.

Delores (Dee) Conway, CLG Principal

Dee Conway is an accomplished, results-oriented leader with twenty years of excellence and increasing responsibility within a Fortune 150 organization. Innovative, focused, and energetic, she is respected for her operational expertise, leadership development, and executive coaching. Her varied background gives her the uncanny ability to analyze issues from multiple perspectives and forge creative solutions to organizational challenges. Dee attended Florida A&M University and the University of Hartford.

Les Dakens, Maple Leaf Foods—SVP and CHRO

Les Dakens is widely recognized in North America as one of the top HR professionals for his leadership in developing best practices. With thirty years of experience working with top-tier companies, he currently oversees executive leadership for all HR development programs and employee relations initiatives at Maple Leaf Foods. Les holds a degree from York University and is a graduate of the Institute of Corporate Directors' Directors Education Program.

Danielle Geissler, PhD, CLG Senior Consultant

Danielle Geissler is a collaborative, passionate consultant and executive coach known for building lasting relationships with clients at all organizational levels. Her specialties include leadership development, performance management, and internal consultant development. Noted for her engaging presentation skills, Danielle is a frequent presenter at conferences. She holds a PhD in Applied Behavior Analysis, with a focus on Organizational Behavior Management, from the City University of New York.

Karen Gorman, CLG Senior Partner

Karen Gorman has more than three decades of experience helping leaders manage change, increase their leadership effectiveness, and achieve sustainable performance results. Articulate and creative, she coaches her clients in using ABS to energize business strategies. As an expert in performance improvement (most notably in manufacturing), Karen has received multiple awards for organizational effectiveness. She is a graduate of the University of Delaware and a published author.

James S. Hillgren, PhD, CLG Partner

Jim Hillgren specialized in helping clients increase their competitive performance. With a comfortable and inviting style, he worked with executives to implement the unique practices of sustained high-performance organizations. An entertaining and engaging speaker, Jim held a doctorate in Clinical Psychology and was codeveloper of CLG's DCOM framework. This and his many other contributions left a lasting impact on CLG. Jim passed away in October 2011.

Deborah K. Kramer, CPA, CLG Partner

Debbie Kramer is a veteran C-suite leader and coach, regarded for working fluidly with all organizational levels to achieve desired results. With her engaging style and keen business acumen, she helps leaders identify key issues and ways to address them strategically and operationally. Prior to joining CLG, Debbie held successive SVP roles over Marketing, HR, and Organizational Development for a Fortune 300 company. She earned her degree from Indiana University.

Vikesh Mahendroo, MA, MBA, CLG President and CEO

Vikesh Mahendroo is a perceptive leader with nearly three decades of experience leading professional-services organizations. He is passionate about helping clients understand and address ever-evolving challenges, developing talent to address those challenges, and focusing their efforts, leadership, and resources in areas important for growth and success. Vikesh received his bachelor's and master's in Economics from St. Stephen's College at Delhi University and his MBA from Columbia University.

Mona Malone, VP HR, Personal and Commercial Banking Canada—Bank of Montreal

Mona Malone's career at Bank of Montreal has encompassed a wide range of areas of expertise, including human resources, advanced leadership and management development programs, design and development of learning initiatives, risk and regulatory issues, and personal and commercial banking. She also specializes in organizational strategy and transformational change. Mona received her HBA from Ivey Business School at University of Western Ontario.

Laura Methot, PhD, CLG Partner

Laura Methot's passion and expertise are in helping organizations expand their leadership capabilities to create conditions for successful business execution. Recognized as a leading behavior analyst, the impact of her work is evident in bottom-line business results and how her clients across multiple industries talk of tangible culture change and leadership effectiveness as a result of working with her. Laura holds a PhD in Applied Behavior Analysis from Western Michigan University.

Annemarie Michaud, MBA, CLG Senior Partner

Annemarie Michaud has nearly three decades of experience with leaders in corporate settings, with over twenty of those years in coaching Fortune 100 executives. In addition to her proactive, get-it-done style, she possesses a deep understanding of organizational change, a portfolio of successful client interventions, and a command of four languages. She earned her MBA from Georgia State University and Professional Certified Coach credential with the International Coach Federation.

Bridget J. Hayes Russell, EdD, CLG Senior Consultant
Bridget Russell is an expert in ABS, performer and consultant development, and performance improvement. Known for her friendly, practical approach, she leads CLG's internal ABS certification program, ensuring that the company's consultants and support staff are well versed in ABS knowledge and application of its principles and methodologies. Bridget holds a doctorate in Educational Psychology with an emphasis in Applied Behavior Analysis from West Virginia University.

Julie M. Smith, PhD, CLG Cofounder
Julie Smith is a world-class coach and international thought leader in behavior-based strategy execution and change leadership. Noted for her astonishing energy and ability to help leaders achieve "mission impossible," she pioneered the integration of Applied Behavioral Science, process improvement, and balanced scorecards for several Fortune 500 companies. An accomplished speaker, author, entrepreneur, and board member, Julie earned her doctorate in Behavior Analysis from West Virginia University.

Tracy Thurkow, PhD, CLG Partner
Tracy Thurkow is an esteemed thought leader on the behavioral implications of transformational change, as well as a highly sought adviser and coach to senior leaders. She makes a point of getting to know clients by understanding their companies inside and out, and her work has improved many premier organizations' capability to execute strategic change through CLG's innovative methods. Tracy holds a doctorate in Industrial/Organizational Psychology from Auburn University.

Elise Walton, PhD, CLG Senior Partner

Elise Walton has many years of rich experience consulting to large, global organizations at the highest levels on critical business challenges they face. In addition to her expertise in corporate governance, CEO succession, and board assessment, her specialties include large-scale change initiatives and change management, executive and leadership development, and strategic organization assessment, design, and alignment. Elise holds a PhD in Organizational Behavior from Harvard University.

ABOUT CLG

The Continuous Learning Group, Inc. (CLG), cofounded in 1993 by Dr. Leslie Braksick, Dr. Julie Smith, and Larry Lemasters, has grown into the largest behaviorally based management-consulting firm in the world. CLG's clients come from the Fortune 500—along with non-US clients of similar size.

CLG offers a consulting partnership that has a lifelong impact on its clients, their people, and their organizations. CLG achieves this by applying the science of behavior to clients' most pressing business challenges and opportunities.

Most clients employ one of CLG's three centerline offers, or some combination of them: Leadership Catalyst^{SM}, Performance Catalyst$^©$, or Change Catalyst^{SM}. CLG begins with the client's need and desired outcomes, and then applies world-class talent and tools to help the client navigate successfully through change, while unlocking and unleashing the organization's discretionary performance.

CLG's consultants work comfortably side by side with leaders at all levels, in the trenches, sweating the same details of getting results that the firm's clients do, taking time to build relationships that deliver results.

CLG's work with CEOs and their boards on issues of CEO succession, executive leadership development, and strategic talent management are heralded by clients who turn to CLG for help in those areas. Similarly, CLG coaches are often found at the business-unit-president and site levels, working with high-potential leaders at all levels to maximize their leadership excellence in areas of greatest importance to the business.

CLG is an enterprise of uncommon people who perform uncommonly well. For a decade and a half, CLG has helped clients achieve remarkable—and measurable—results in ways that also develop sturdy, positive, high-performing cultures. CLG helps execute the behavioral portion of clients' most challenging strategies. CLG helps clients whenever leadership excellence, changing behavior, and emotional engagement are critical to achieving business results.

To discover more, visit www.clg.com or call 800-887-0011 x 2038.

ALSO FROM OUR CLG COLLEAGUES

Unlock Behavior, Unleash Profits: Developing Leadership Behavior that Drives Profitability in Your Organization, Leslie Wilk Braksick, PhD

Summary: This book gives away tools and methods used by the largest behaviorally based management consulting firm in the world—CLG (www.clg.com). It is filled with client stories, case studies, testimonials, and—most important—the secrets to what has led to personal and organizational transformations in blue-chip companies: behavioral science applied to business.

Preparing CEOs for Success, Leslie W. Braksick, PhD, James S. Hillgren, PhD

Summary: Chief Executive Officer William R. Johnson of the H. J. Heinz Company, in support of his own CEO succession planning and development efforts, sponsored the research project that prompted publication of this book. The work was made possible by the participation and remarkable candor of Bill and twenty-six other sitting CEOs of global companies. Drs. Leslie W. Braksick and James S. Hillgren of the Continuous Learning Group conducted the research during 2008 and 2009. The purpose of the research is to provide unvarnished advice based on the real experiences of sitting CEOs to assist in preparing future CEOs, executives, and leaders. Often, the participants' experiences were unflattering to themselves or their companies, and yet they shared openly and honestly with the assurance of confidentiality. It matters not who said what, but rather that an impressive collection of CEO peers offered these important insights for future peer CEOs.

SwitchPoints: Culture Change on the Fast Track to Business Success, Judy Johnson, PhD, Les Dakens, Peter Edwards, Ned Morse

Summary: *SwitchPoints* is the inspiring story of how Canadian National Railway (CN) advanced from good to great in a few short years—becoming North America's top-performing railroad and a favorite with corporate customers and investors. In this book, the authors reveal how company-wide culture change propelled this aging transportation giant to become the profitable powerhouse it is today. Rich with insights and anecdotes, *SwitchPoints* offers lessons that can be applied to any organization seeking to improve the bottom line by improving their culture.

INDEX